AQA (A) AS

UNIT

2

Psychology

...logical Psychology, Social Psychology
...Individual Differences

...olly Marshall

Philip Allan Updates, an imprint of Hodder Education, part of Hachette Livre UK, Market Place, Deddington, Oxfordshire OX15 0SE

Orders

Bookpoint Ltd, 130 Milton Park, Abingdon, Oxfordshire, OX14 4SB
tel: 01235 827720
fax: 01235 400454
e-mail: uk.orders@bookpoint.co.uk

Lines are open 9.00 a.m.–5.00 p.m., Monday to Saturday, with a 24-hour message answering service. You can also order through the Philip Allan Updates website: www.philipallan.co.uk

© Philip Allan Updates 2008

ISBN 978-0-340-96673-0

First printed 2008
Impression number 5 4 3 2 1
Year 2013 2012 2011 2010 2009 2008

This guide has been written specifically to support students preparing for Specification A AS Psychology Unit 2 examination. The content has been approved nor endorsed by AQA and remains the sole responsibility of the au

Printed by MPG Books, Bodmin

Hachette Livre UK's policy is to use papers that are natural, renewable and recycl products and made from wood grown in sustainable forests. The logging manufacturing processes are expected to conform to the environmental regulatt of the country of origin.

Contents

Introduction

About this guide

This is a guide to Unit 2 of AQA(A) AS Psychology. Unit 2 examines **biological psychology**, **social psychology** and **individual differences**. The guide is intended as a revision *aid* rather than as a textbook or revision guide. It focuses on how the specification content is examined and how different answers to sample questions may be assessed.

The three sections of biological psychology, social psychology and individual differences are covered, and for each of these sections the following are provided:
- the specification content for each topic, so that you know what you may be asked to demonstrate in an exam
- appropriate content relevant to each topic — as *minimal* coverage for each topic area. This is not intended as the *only* appropriate content for a given topic, but gives you an idea of what you might include and how you might present an answer to a question on a particular aspect of the specification.
- a glossary of key terms, constructed to be succinct but informative
- examples of questions in the style of AQA(A) AS examination questions. Each is accompanied by a full explanation of its requirements as well as the appropriate breakdown of marks between AO1, AO2 and AO3 skills.
- an example of a B/C/D-grade response to each of these questions, with comments showing where marks have been gained or lost
- an example of an A-grade response to each of these questions, showing how the question might be answered by a strong candidate

How to use this guide

This guide is *not* intended as a set of model answers to possible examination questions, or as an account of the right material to include in any examination question. It is intended to give you an idea of how your examination is structured and how you might improve your examination performance.

You should read through the relevant topic in the Content Guidance before you attempt a question from the Question and Answer section. Look at the sample answers only after you have tackled the question yourself.

The examination

Assessment objectives: AO1, AO2 and AO3 skills

AO1	Recognise, recall and show understanding of scientific knowledge, select, organise and communicate relevant information in a variety of forms.
AO2	Analyse and evaluate scientific knowledge, apply knowledge and processes to unfamiliar situations, assess the validity, reliability and credibility of scientific information.
AO3	Describe ethical, safe and skilful practical techniques and processes, know how to make, record and communicate valid observations, analyse, interpret, explain and evaluate the methodology and investigative activities in a variety of forms.

Unit·2 is assessed in an examination lasting 1 hour 30 minutes and you must answer all the questions. Section A comprises questions on biological psychology, Section B has questions on social psychology and Section C contains questions on individual differences.

Questions

The following are examples of the types of question that may be used to assess your AO1, AO2 and AO3 skills.

AO1 questions

Outline the effect that stress may have on the immune system. *(6 marks)*

Outline the use of drugs in the control of stress. *(4 marks)*

Outline what is meant by normative social influence. *(4 marks)*

Outline key features of the psychodynamic approach to psychopathology. *(6 marks)*

AO2 questions

Evaluate the use of psychological treatment to manage the negative effects of stress.
(8 marks)

Explain the difference between normative and informational social influence.
(3 marks)

Explain how psychological research helps us to understand why people are influenced by others. *(6 marks)*

Explain how systematic desensitisation may overcome a fear of flying. *(6 marks)*

Discuss the extent to which drug treatment is an effective and appropriate way to treat mental disorders. *(6 marks)*

AO1 + AO2 questions

Discuss the view that stress is environmentally determined. *(12 marks)*

Describe and evaluate research into social influence. *(12 marks)*

AO3 questions

Discuss the methodological problems faced by social psychologists who conduct research in a laboratory. *(5 marks)*

Discuss one ethical issue raised by the Milgram research. *(4 marks)*

Explain one way that psychologists have investigated the genetic basis of abnormality. *(4 marks)*

Effective examination performance

Read the question carefully because marks are only awarded for the specific requirements of the question *as it is set*. Do not waste valuable time answering a question that you wish had been set.

Make a brief plan before you start writing an extended answer. This plan can be a simple list of points, but you must know what, and how much, you plan to write. Time management in exams is vital.

Sometimes a question asks you to *outline* something. You should practise doing this in order to develop the skill of précis, which is not as easy as it sounds.

Be aware of the difference between AO1, AO2 and AO3 questions. You will lose marks if you treat AO2 questions as an opportunity to write more descriptive (AO1) content. Read the question injunction carefully and note the relevant skill requirement in your question plan (e.g. outline = AO1, describe = AO1, evaluate = AO2, discuss = marks are split between AO1 and AO2).

In AO1 questions, marks are awarded in bands for the quality of relevant material presented (e.g. low marks for brief or inappropriate; high marks for accurate and detailed).

In AO2 questions and/or the AO2 component of AO1 + AO2 questions, marks are awarded in bands for the amount, quality and effectiveness of critical commentary (e.g. low marks for superficial consideration of a restricted range of issues; high marks for a good range of ideas and specialist terms and effective use of material addressing a broad range of issues).

AO3 questions require you to demonstrate a thorough understanding of methods by which psychologists conduct research. You must:

- be able to describe ethical, safe and skilful practical techniques and processes
- know how to make, record and communicate valid observations
- be able to analyse, interpret, explain and evaluate methodology and investigative activities

How the marks are awarded

Mark allocations for an AO1/AO2/AO3 12-mark question

Example

Discuss the view that stress is environmentally determined.   *(12 marks)*

Marks criteria for AO1 + AO2 + AO3

AO1 Knowledge and understanding	AO2 and AO3 Application of knowledge and understanding
6 marks: accurate and reasonably detailed Accurate and reasonably detailed description of (environmental determinants of stress) that demonstrates sound knowledge and understanding of relevant research. There is appropriate selection of material to address the question.	**6 marks: effective evaluation** Effective use of material to address the question and provide informed commentary. Effective evaluation of research. Broad range of issues and/or evidence in reasonable depth, or a narrower range in greater depth. Clear expression of ideas, good range of specialist terms, few errors of grammar, punctuation or spelling.
5–4 marks: less detailed but generally accurate Less detailed but generally accurate description that demonstrates relevant knowledge and understanding of research. There is some evidence of selection of material to address the question.	**5–4 marks: reasonable evaluation** Material is not always used effectively but a reasonable commentary is produced. Reasonable evaluation of research. A range of issues and/or evidence in limited depth, or a narrower range in greater depth. Reasonable expression of ideas, a range of specialist terms, some errors of grammar, punctuation and spelling.
3–2 marks: basic Basic description that demonstrates some relevant knowledge and understanding but lacks detail and may be muddled. There is little evidence of selection of material to address the question.	**3–2 marks: basic evaluation** Use of material provides only a basic commentary. Basic evaluation of research. Superficial consideration of a restricted range of issues and/or evidence. Expression of ideas lacks clarity, some specialist terms used, errors of grammar, punctuation and spelling detract from clarity.
1 mark: very brief/flawed or inappropriate Very brief or flawed description demonstrating very little knowledge. Selection and presentation of information is largely or wholly inappropriate.	**1 mark: rudimentary evaluation** The use of material provides only a rudimentary commentary. Evaluation of research is just discernible or absent. Expression of ideas poor, few specialist terms used, errors of grammar, punctuation and spelling often obscure the meaning.
0 marks: no creditworthy material.	**0 marks: no creditworthy material.**

Mark allocations for an AO1 6-mark question

Example

Outline key features of the psychodynamic approach to psychopathology. *(6 marks)*

Marks criteria for AO1

Marks	Recognise, recall and show understanding of scientific knowledge; select, organise and communicate relevant information
6	Accurate and reasonably detailed outline of (*key features of the psychodynamic approach*) that demonstrates sound knowledge and understanding of (*key features of the psychodynamic approach*) and appropriate selection of material.
5–4	Less detailed but generally accurate outline of (*key features of the psychodynamic approach*) that demonstrates knowledge and understanding and some evidence of selection of material.
3–2	Basic outline of (*key features of the psychodynamic approach*) and limited evidence of selection of material.
1	Brief or flawed outline of (*key features of the psychodynamic approach*) demonstrating very little knowledge.
0	No creditworthy material.

How marks are awarded for an AO2 6-mark question

Example

Explain how psychological research helps us to understand why people are influenced by others. *(6 marks)*

Marks criteria for AO2

Marks	Analyse and evaluate scientific knowledge; apply knowledge and processes to unfamiliar situations; assess the validity, reliability and credibility of scientific information
6	**Effective evaluation:** effective use of material, broad range of issues and/or evidence in reasonable depth or narrower range of issues in greater depth, good range of specialist terms, clear expression of ideas, few errors of grammar, spelling or punctuation.
5–4	**Reasonable evaluation:** material used less effectively but a range of issues/ evidence in limited depth or fewer issues in greater depth, a range of specialist terms, some errors of grammar, punctuation or spelling.
3–2	**Basic evaluation:** superficial consideration of a limited range of issues and/or evidence, lack of clarity in use of specialist terms or spelling, punctuation or grammar errors detract from clarity.
1	**Rudimentary evaluation:** evaluation of material is just discernible, expression of ideas is poor, few specialist terms.
0	**No creditworthy material presented**

Content Guidance

This section gives content guidance on the topics of biological psychology (stress), social psychology (social influence) and individual differences (psychopathology).

Each part-topic begins with an outline of the AQA specification A requirement. This is followed by a more detailed look at the theories and studies that comprise the Unit 2 content.

Knowledge of appropriate theories, studies and research methods is essential for the AS examination. It is also important to be able to assess the value of these theories, studies and research methods.

At the end of each topic a glossary of key terms is provided — those terms that you will need to use, or may be asked to define, in an examination.

Names and publication dates have been given when referring to research studies. The full references for these studies should be available in textbooks should you wish to read about or research the topic further.

Biological psychology: stress
Stress as a bodily response

Specification content

- the body's response to stress, including the pituitary-adrenal system and the sympathomedullary pathway (in outline)
- the relationship between stress and physical illness, including the effects of stress on the immune system

Physiological psychology focuses on biological explanations of behaviour, such as how and why the brain and nervous system respond to stressors.

What is stress?

You need to know how the body responds to stressors, for example the role of the **autonomic nervous system** and the **pituitary-adrenal system**. You also need to be able to describe and evaluate research into the relationship between stress and illness and the effect of stress on the **immune system**. In terms of stress in everyday life you need to be able to describe and evaluate research into the **sources of stress**. You also need to understand that there are different ways by which stress can be managed and you need to be able to describe and evaluate **physiological** and **psychological approaches** to managing stress.

Stress is a type of alarm reaction, involving heightened mental and bodily states. It is both a psychological and a physiological response to the environment. Your brain produces a stress reaction when you are in a situation that is physically or mentally demanding. Thus, stress can be defined as the response that happens when **we think we cannot cope** with a stressor in the environment. If we think we cannot cope, we feel stress, and when we feel stress, we experience physiological changes.

The hypothalamic-pituitary-adrenal axis

The stress response originates in the hypothalamus and includes the pituitary and adrenal glands. This hypothalamic-pituitary-adrenal axis is responsible for arousing the autonomic nervous system (ANS) in response to a stressor.

Under stress, the sympathetic branch of the nervous system stimulates the adrenal gland to release adrenaline, noradrenaline and corticosteroids into the bloodstream. This produces the physiological reactions, such as increased heart rate and blood pressure and a dry mouth, known as the 'fight or flight' response.

The general adaptation syndrome (GAS)

Selye (1956) proposed that stress leads to a depletion of the body's resources, leaving the animal vulnerable to illness. He used the word 'stress' to describe the fact that many different stimuli (fear, pain, injury) all produce the same response. He called these 'stressors' and proposed that the body reacts in the same general way to all these stressors by producing a response which helps the animal adapt to them and continue to function. Selye called this the 'general adaptation syndrome' (GAS) and identified three stages in the model.

Stage 1, alarm. When we perceive a stressor, the ANS responds. Adrenaline, noradrenaline and corticosteroids (hormones) are released into the bloodstream. The bodily reaction is increased arousal levels in readiness for a physical response (fight or flight), i.e. the heart rate increases, blood pressure rises and muscles tense.

Stage 2, resistance. If the stressor continues, the bodily reaction (the fight or flight response) ceases and we appear to be coping. But output from the adrenal cortex continues and the adrenal glands may become enlarged.

Stage 3, exhaustion. If the stressor continues for a long time, the body is unable to cope. The body's resources are reduced but alarm signs, such as increased blood pressure, may return. The person may become depressed and unable to concentrate. The immune system may be damaged and stress-related diseases, such as stomach ulcers, high blood pressure and depression, are more likely to occur.

Stress-related illness

Stress and cardiovascular disorders

Cardiovascular disorders are disorders of the heart and blood vessels and are sometimes linked with stress. People who experience stress may engage in unhealthy activities, such as smoking and drinking alcohol, in an attempt to relieve the stress. These behaviours increase the likelihood that the person may develop a cardiovascular disorder, so stress may cause illness indirectly.

Long-term stress may also have a direct effect on the cardiovascular system. Stress causes high heart rate and high blood pressure. Long-term stress can damage blood vessels because adrenaline and noradrenaline contribute to increases in blood cholesterol levels, leading to blood clots and thickened arteries. Weakened or damaged blood vessels may cause haemorrhages, which in turn may lead to blockages in blood vessels, causing strokes or heart attacks.

The effect of stress on blood flow (Krantz et al. 1991)

In this study, the direct effect of stress on blood flow and blood pressure was investigated. Thirty-nine participants performed a stress-inducing task (e.g. a maths test) while their blood pressure and rate of blood flow to the heart were measured. The stressful task caused a reduced blood flow to the heart and led to raised blood pressure. From this it was concluded that stress does have a direct effect on the cardiovascular system, making cardiovascular disorders more likely.

Type A personality (Friedman and Rosenman 1974)

Cardiologists Friedman and Rosenman defined two types of behaviour pattern, Type A and Type B, and studied their relation to coronary heart disease.

Type A behaviour: Type A people move, walk, eat and talk rapidly, and try to do two or more things at one time. In personality, Type A people are competitive and tend to judge themselves by the number of successes they have rather than the quality of their successes. Type A individuals are hard-driving, impatient and aggressive. They tend to be achievement-oriented and hostile. In physiology, Type A people have a higher level of cholesterol and fat in their bloodstream, a more difficult time getting the cholesterol out of their bloodstream, and a greater likelihood of clotting within the arteries.

Type B behaviour: Type B people seldom feel any sense of time urgency or impatience, are not preoccupied with their achievements or accomplishments and seldom become angry or irritable. They tend to enjoy their recreation, are free of guilt about relaxing, and they work calmly and smoothly.

Type A personality (Friedman and Rosenman 1974)

Aim: Based on their observations of patients who displayed the common Type A behaviour pattern of impatience, competitiveness and hostility, Friedman and Rosenman aimed to test their belief that Type A personalities were more prone to coronary heart disease (CHD) than Type B personalities.

Procedures: The sample comprised 3,000 male volunteers, all from California, USA, aged between 39 and 59, who were healthy at the start of the study. Personality type was established through the use of a structured interview and observations of the participants' behaviour during the interview. The interviewer interrupted the interview from time to time so that the Type A individuals would become annoyed. The answers to questions and behavioural responses were used to assess participants' impatience, competitiveness and hostility.

Findings: $8\frac{1}{2}$ years later, 257 of the men in the sample were diagnosed as having CHD. Seventy per cent of those with CHD had been classified as Type A.

The Type A men were also found to have higher levels of adrenaline and cholesterol. Twice as many Type A men had died as compared with Type Bs. Type As also had higher blood pressure, higher cholesterol and other symptoms of CHD. Type As were more likely to smoke and have a family history of CHD, both of which would increase their own risk.

Conclusion: Type A personality is associated with illness and symptoms of CHD. Because Type A is also linked to other factors that cause CHD, such as smoking, it is not certain whether Type A is a direct or indirect cause of CHD.

Criticisms

- The study has high external validity because it was a long-term study with a large sample having a baseline measure (all the men were free of CHD at the start of the study).
- The study is useful because it showed how psychological factors (personality) are related to physiological factors (CHD).
- The study cannot show that Type A personality causes CHD. It may be that Type A behaviours develop as a result of long-term stress.
- Categorising all men into two personality types is reductionist. Later research has identified Type C and D personalities.
- The sample was both ethnocentric and gender-biased (all males from the USA) and as such cannot be generalised to females.
- The findings of Williams (2000) support Friedman and Rosenman in their description of Type A personalities as hostile. In Williams's study, 13,000 participants completed questionnaires asking about their feelings of anger, and the participants' responses were rated for anger scores. Six years later, those with high anger scores were significantly more likely to have suffered a heart attack.

Stress and the immune system

The immune system comprises billions of cells that travel through the bloodstream. They are produced in the bone marrow, spleen, lymph nodes and thymus. The major type of immune cell is the white blood cell, which defends the body against antigens — bacteria, viruses and cancerous cells. Some types of immune cells produce antibodies that destroy antigens. When we are stressed, the ability of the immune system to protect us against antigens is reduced, leading to an increased likelihood of physical illness. This weakening of the immune system is called the **immuno-suppressive effect of stress**. In long-term stress, such as stage 3 of Selye's GAS, increased levels of corticosteroids reduce the production of antibodies (a direct effect).

Stress and the immune system (Kiecolt-Glaser et al. 1984)

Based on the assumption that the body's response to stress reduces the effectiveness of the immune system (immunosuppression), Kiecolt-Glaser et al. aimed to establish a link between stress and reduced immune system functioning.

Aims: To look for evidence of a difference in immune response in high- and low-stress conditions, and to see whether factors such as anxiety were associated with immune system functioning.

Procedures: 75 first-year medical students (49 male and 26 female) volunteered to give blood samples 1 month before their final exams, and again after they had sat two papers on the first day of the exams. The blood samples were analysed for how much 'natural killer cell' activity was present (natural killer cells help to protect against viruses). The students also completed questionnaires to find out what other stressful events they might be experiencing.

Findings: In comparison with the first blood sample, natural killer cell activity was significantly reduced in the second sample. It was most reduced in those students who were experiencing other stressful events, and in those who reported feeling anxious and depressed.

Conclusion: Stress has an immunosuppressant effect and can be associated with reduced immune system function.

Criticisms
- The study has high external realism as the exams were real-life experiences and would have happened anyway.
- The first blood sample acted as a baseline control and the participants were being compared against themselves — this controlled for the effects of personality variables.
- It is not possible to exclude other factors that could have caused the change in the students' immune systems as other variables could not be controlled (e.g. it might have been lack of sleep due to long hours revising that affected the immune system).
- It is not possible to say how long-lasting the reduced effectiveness of the immune system might be.

The effect of stress on wound healing (Kiecolt-Glaser et al. 1995)

The immune system is involved in helping the body repair itself after injury. Following tissue damage (cuts and wounds), the immune system produces interleukin B that promotes healing by helping to create scar tissue.

Aim: To show that stress has an indirect effect on wound healing due to reduced effectiveness of the immune system.

Procedures: The study involved 13 women who cared for relatives suffering from Alzheimer's disease (the high-stress group), and a control group of 13 women who had no stressful responsibilities (the no-stress group). All the women gave skin samples, which caused skin wounds.

Findings: The wounds of the carers in the high-stress group took, on average, 9 days longer than those of the no-stress group to heal. It was concluded that long-term stress reduces the effectiveness of the immune system to heal wounds.

Criticisms
- The study is useful to National Health Service staff as it may explain why the wounds of some patients take longer to heal than expected.
- The sample was small and all female, and it may not be safe to generalise the findings to other populations.
- There was no baseline measure of how rapidly the wounds might have healed in the high-stress group before the onset of the stressor.

Stress in everyday life

Specification content

You need to be able to describe, evaluate and understand research into the following:
- *sources of stress, including life changes and daily hassles, workplace stress, and personality factors, including Type A behaviour*
- *emotion-focused and problem-focused approaches to coping with stress*
- *methods of managing stress, including physiological treatments and psychological approaches*

Sources of stress

Two major sources of stress are changes in an individual's life, and work.

Life events. Throughout our lives we experience many changes, such as leaving home, marriage, changing employment, the birth of children and moving house. These events cause us to change the way we live, and adjusting to change may cause stress.

The workplace. Work can be stressful. For some people, the kind of work they do, where they work and with whom they work can be a source of stress. Some of the more stressful occupations are nursing, teaching and the emergency services. Someone who is stressed at work may become ill and need to take time off.

However, there are also **individual differences:** no two people respond to stressors in the same way. Some people seem to thrive on lifestyles that others would find stressful. Psychologists research how **personality factors** may be involved in how people respond to stressors.

Life changes and the Social Readjustment Rating Scale (SRRS) (Holmes and Rahe 1967)

Aims:

(1) To construct an instrument for measuring stress (stress was defined as the amount of life change people had experienced during a fixed period).

(2) To show that the amount of life change (i.e. the amount of stress) is related to psychological and physiological illness.

Procedures: The medical records of 5,000 patients were examined and a list was compiled of 43 kinds of life event that had taken place in the 12 months before their illnesses. One hundred people (the 'judges') were told that the life event of marriage had been rated at 500 points. They were then asked to rate how much readjustment each of the 43 life events would require 'relative to marriage'.

Findings:

(1) Death of a spouse was thought to require twice as much adjustment as marriage and was rated at 1,000 points by the judges. The average for each of the 43 life events was calculated. Holmes and Rahe could now rank the 43 life events from death of a spouse (at 1,000 points) to minor violations of the law (11 points), resulting in their Social Readjustment Rating Scale. A questionnaire was designed in which participants ticked the life events they had experienced in the last 12 months, thus giving a measure of the amount of life change (stress) they had experienced.

(2) People with high scores on the SRRS (over the previous 12 months) were likely to experience some physical illness. A person having 300 points over 12 months had an 80% chance of becoming ill, and illnesses ranged from heart attacks to diabetes and sports injuries.

Conclusions

(1) Stress can be objectively measured by the SRRS as a life change score.

(2) High scores on the SRRS (high-stress scores) predict physical illness, and stressful life changes cause physical illness.

Criticisms

- The research provides an objective measure of the relationship between stress and illness. Supporting evidence was found from a study in which 2500 navy personnel completed the SRRS before they left for a 6-month trip on board their ships. Health records were kept which found that high scores on the SRRS were correlated with physical illness.

- The experience of a life event is different for each person; for example, some people may be distressed by divorce whereas others are relieved. Life events other than the 43 on the SRRS may also cause stress, for example having your home flooded.

> • Most of the 43 life events are infrequent and the daily small hassles of life may be a more significant cause of stress.

Daily hassles and stress (DeLongis et al. 1982)

DeLongis et al. theorised that it was everyday hassles that caused stress. They created a hassles scale to assess the effect of the routine problems of life, such as getting stuck in a traffic jam. The hassles scale measures positive events (uplifts) as well as hassles. In people over 45, they found that the hassles scale was a better predictor of ill health than life changes (SRRS). The frequency and intensity of hassles significantly correlated to ill health.

Workplace stress: sources of stress

Stress in the workplace can originate in **six areas**:

(1) **Interpersonal factors**. Relationships with bosses, colleagues and customers may be stressful. Social support is important in moderating the effects of stress in general. Good relationships with co-workers can reduce stress in the workplace; poor relationships at work can exacerbate stress.

(2) **Work pressure.** Having too much work to do and working to strict deadlines can cause stress.

(3) **The physical environment.** This may be noisy, hot and overcrowded, or may involve health risks and unsociable hours, such as working night shifts. Czeisler et al. (1982) researched the causes of health problems and sleep difficulties experienced by employees of a chemical plant in Utah, USA. The employees worked shifts. Czeisler recommended that the pattern of shifts should be changed to a 21-day shift rotation and always 'shift forward' (phase advance). After 9 months, job satisfaction and productivity increased.

(4) **Role stress.** Worry about job security or responsibility may cause stress.

(5) **Role conflict.** Having to express one emotion while feeling another may cause stress, e.g. in doctors, nurses, police.

(6) **Control.** How much control people have over how they do a job may be a factor in how stressful the job is perceived to be.

Research into control and interpersonal relationships at work (Johnson and Hall 1988)

Aim: To investigate the relationship between variables in the workplace (social support, perceived control and how demanding jobs are) and the incidence of cardiovascular disease.

Procedures: Data from 14,000 male and female Swedish workers were analysed to explore the relationship between cardiovascular disease and job stress, specifically stress associated with control, demand and social support. The data included four scales of measurement:

(1) work control, based on questions about the level of influence over the planning of work

(2) work-related social support, based on questions about how and when workers could interact with co-workers

(3) psychological demands of work, based on questions about how demanding the work was

(4) an indicator of cardiovascular health

Findings:

- Jobs that were perceived to be demanding but that involved low levels of control were related to increased incidences of heart disease.
- Where workers had fewer social interaction opportunities (low social support), there was an increase in cardiovascular disease in the high-demand, high-control combination.
- Low social support combined with low control increased cardiovascular disease.

Conclusion: Both social support and control are important factors in work-related stress.

Criticisms

- This research is useful because it shows how factors such as control and social support at work are important in understanding workplace stress.
- Self-reports may result in inaccurate descriptions of job characteristics and may be biased by personality characteristics.
- Workplaces are complex. Using objective measures of workplace stress may result in a reductionist approach that overemphasises the social context of stress.
- Qualitative research is required in order to understand the meaning of events for individuals.

Research into factors that may cause stress in the workplace

Role conflict in the workplace (Margolis and Kroes 1974)

This research found that when the demands of the organisation conflict with the needs of the workers, stress may result. They found that when the job requires workers to express one emotion, e.g. being calm and cheerful, while really feeling another emotion, e.g. being unhappy or worried, this causes role conflict. Nurses, teachers and paramedics are likely to suffer stress caused by role conflict.

Is having control at work important? (Marmot et al. 1997)

This research investigated whether perceived control is an important factor in work-related stress. In their study, 7,000 civil service employees who worked in London participated in a survey. Data were gathered on how senior they were (their employment grade) and how much control and support they perceived they had at work. Five years later, the medical histories of the employees were reviewed. The participants who were less senior (lower grades) and who felt they had less control and less social support were more likely to have cardiovascular disorders. It was concluded that how much control people have at work, and how much social support people receive from colleagues, may be factors in whether they suffer from stress-related illness.

Individual differences in response to stressors

Personality differences and stress

The Type A personality, especially the hostile Type A personality, is significantly associated with coronary heart disease. The Type C personality, hardworking, conventional and sociable, responds to stress with a sense of helplessness and may be more likely to suffer from cancer. In support of this, Morris et al. (1981) found a link between people who tended to suppress their anger and the increased incidence of cancer.

Helgeson and Fritz (1999) studied nearly 300 patients receiving treatment for blocked arteries. Six months later, they found that those patients who were lowest in 'cognitive adaptation' were three times more likely to have experienced a new coronary event. High cognitive adaptation included an ability to develop a positive outlook about one's medical condition and a sense of control in most situations. They concluded that the 'pessimist personality' is more likely to become ill as a result of stress.

Kobasa (1979) proposed that some people are better able to deal with stress (the hardy personality) and that all people could learn to behave in this way in order to cope better. The key traits of a hardy personality, known as the three Cs, are having a strong sense of personal *control*, a strong sense of purpose (*commitment*) and the ability to see problems positively, as *challenges* to be overcome rather than as stressors.

Gender differences and stress

More men suffer from coronary heart disease than women, and there are several explanations as to why gender may be an important factor in stress:

- women are biologically more able to cope with stress
- women are socialised to cope better with stress
- women tend to drink and smoke less and may do less stressful work

From an **evolutionary (biological) perspective**, men should respond to situations of danger with the 'fight or flight' arousal response, whereas women should respond by looking after young ones and each other. **Taylor et al. (2000)** reviewed many biological and behavioural studies (both human and animal) and concluded that females were more likely to deal with stress by nurturing those around them and reaching out to others. Men were more likely to hide away or start a confrontation. This suggests different responses to stress which match gender types.

From a **social perspective**, males and females are socialised in different ways. Women learn to use social networks more and this may reduce their stress. They are taught to think about social conflict situations differently. **Vögele et al. (1997)** proposed that females learn to control their anger and react more calmly in stressful situations, but males learn that anger is an acceptable response and feel stress if they have to suppress anger. **Iso et al. (2002)** looked at 73,000 white Japanese male and female participants aged 40–79. Participants were asked to rate the level of stress in their daily lives. Over the following 8 years, those Japanese women who reported high levels of stress were more than twice as likely to die from stroke and heart disease as women reporting low stress levels. Moreover, perceived mental stress was associated with increased death from stroke for women, and with CHD in men and women; overall there was an increase in stress-related risk to health in women. There may also be **gender differences in lifestyles** because women engage in less unhealthy behaviour than men, e.g. they smoke and drink less.

Stress management

Stress management refers to therapies used by doctors in clinical situations and to coping strategies taught by psychologists. It can also refer to the informal ways in which people try to cope with stress in their lives. Psychologists categorise coping strategies as:
* physiological or psychological
* emotion-focused or problem-focused

Physiological approaches to stress management help people cope by changing the way the body responds to stress. They focus on the reduction of physical symptoms of stress.

Psychological approaches to stress management help people cope by getting them to think about their problems in a different way. Such approaches focus on encouraging people to deal with the causes of their stress. One psychological approach is to increase the sense of control people have in stressful situations.

Emotion-focused approaches may attempt to reduce the symptoms of anxiety by taking a physiological approach; for example, biofeedback or anti-anxiety drugs may be used.

Problem-focused approaches attempt to change how people respond to stressors, e.g. by using cognitive therapies or by encouraging people to increase their social support.

It is important to note that emotion-focused and problem-focused approaches are not exclusive categories, as problem-focused approaches also deal with emotions.

Stress management: physiological approaches
Drugs
Drugs aim to reduce the physiological, or bodily, response to stress. Two drugs which do this are benzodiazepine and beta-blockers.

Benzodiazepine is an anti-anxiety (anxiolytic) drug and its brand names include Librium and Valium. These drugs slow down the activity of the central nervous system

(CNS) and reduce anxiety by enhancing the activity of a natural biochemical substance, gamma-amino-butyric-acid (GABA). GABA is the body's natural form of anxiety relief and it also reduces **serotonin** activity. Serotonin is a neurotransmitter and people with anxiety need to reduce their levels of serotonin.

Beta-blockers act on the sympathetic nervous system (SNS) rather than the brain. They reduce heart rate and blood pressure and thus reduce the harmful effects of stress.

Evaluation

Advantages of drugs
- They are quick and effective and reduce the physiological effects of stress.
- People prefer drug therapies to psychological therapies because 'taking a pill is easy'.
- They do not require people to change the way they think or behave.
- They can be used in conjunction with psychological methods.

Limitations of drugs
- All drugs have side effects. Benzodiazepines can cause drowsiness and may affect memory.
- Long-term use of drugs can lead to physical and psychological dependency.
- They treat the symptoms of stress. Most stresses are psychological and drugs do not address the causes of the problem.

Biofeedback

Biofeedback works because our minds can influence the automatic functions of our bodies. Using a special machine, people can learn to control processes such as heart rate and blood pressure. Biofeedback machines provide information about the systems in the body that are affected by stress.

The electromyogram (EMG) measures muscle tension. Electrodes are placed on your skin and when tension is detected, the machine gives you a signal. As you become aware of this internal process, you can learn techniques to control tension. Galvanic skin response (GSR) training devices measure electrical conductance in the skin. A tiny electrical current is run through your skin and the machine measures changes in sweat gland ducts. The more emotionally aroused (stressed) you are, the more active your sweat glands are, and the greater the electrical conductivity of your skin.

There are four stages in learning biofeedback:
- The person is attached to a machine that monitors changes in heart rate and blood pressure and gives feedback.
- The person learns to control the symptoms of stress by deep breathing and muscle relaxation; this slows down their heart rate, making them feel more relaxed.
- The biofeedback from the machine acts like a reward and encourages the person to repeat the breathing techniques.
- Through practice, the person learns to repeat the breathing techniques in stressful situations.

Evaluation

Advantages of biofeedback
- There are no side effects.
- It reduces symptoms and gives people a sense of control.
- The learned techniques can be generalised to other stressful situations.
- It is more effective if combined with psychological therapies that encourage people to think about the causes of their stress and how their behaviour may contribute to it.

Limitations of biofeedback
- It requires specialist equipment and expert supervision.
- It requires the stressed person to commit time and effort.
- Anxious people may find learning biofeedback techniques difficult and it may not be effective therapy for children.

Stress management: psychological approaches

Cognitive Behavioural Therapy (CBT): stress inoculation (Meichenbaum 1985)

The aim of Cognitive Behavioural Therapy is to prepare people to cope with stress in a similar way to an injection preventing a disease. Training people to deal with stress before it becomes a problem involves three stages:

(1) **Conceptualisation.** Patients identify and express their feelings and fears. They are encouraged to imagine stressful situations and analyse what is stressful about them and how they might deal with them.

(2) **Skill acquisition and rehearsal.** Patients practise how to relax and how to express their emotions. Specific skills may be taught, such as positive thinking, communication skills and time management.

(3) **Application and follow-through.** Patients are supported through progressively more threatening real-life situations while applying the newly acquired skills.

Evaluation

Advantages of stress inoculation
- It focuses on the cause of stress and on ways of coping with it.
- It is effective for both short- and long-term stressors and can be combined with other treatment methods.
- The increased feelings of 'being in control' and improved communication and time-management skills lead to increased self-confidence and self-efficacy.
- There are no physiological side effects.

Limitations of stress inoculation
- It may only be successful with patients who are already determined to make the time and effort to help themselves.
- The research findings are based on a narrow sample (mainly white middle-class, well-educated people); thus they may not generalise to other populations.

Increasing hardiness (Kobasa 1977)

The aim of increasing hardiness is to encourage people to respond to stressors in a positive manner instead of perceiving them as disasters, and to teach the behavioural, physiological and cognitive skills that enable them to cope with stressors. Hardiness training involves three stages:

(1) **Focusing.** Patients are taught to recognise the signs of stress, such as muscle tension and tiredness, and to identify the sources of the stress.

(2) **Re-living stressful encounters.** Patients are asked to re-live stressful situations and to analyse these situations so that they can learn from past experience.

(3) **Self-improvement.** Patients use the insights gained to help them see stressors as challenges that can be coped with, leading to improved self-confidence and an enhanced sense of personal control.

Evaluation

Advantages of increasing hardiness

- Evidence suggests this approach is effective. Williams et al. (1992) found that 'high' hardy people use more problem-focused and support-seeking measures when dealing with stress than 'low' hardy people, who tend to use avoidance and wishful thinking. Hardiness is associated with successful coping strategies.
- As with stress inoculation, hardiness training focuses on coping with the causes of stress.
- It can be combined with other treatment methods and improves self-confidence and self-efficacy.

Limitations of increasing hardiness

- The research findings are based on an all-male sample and may not generalise to females.
- It may only be successful with patients who see stress as a challenge to be coped with.
- The concept of hardiness is complex, and in stressful situations even hardy personalities may succumb to anxiety and negative thinking.

Stress management: the role of control

Having a sense of 'being in control' has been shown to reduce stress. Psychological approaches to stress management emphasise taking cognitive control, by thinking positively in order to minimise the effects of stressors.

Locus of control (Rotter 1966)

Rotter categorised people into two types. Those having an **external locus of control** believe that good things happen because of luck, and bad things happen because someone else causes them to. People having an external locus of control perceive they have no control and are likely to become anxious in stressful situations. Those having an **internal locus of control** see themselves as responsible for what happens to them and are more likely to take action to manage stressful situations.

The illusion of control (Glass and Singer 1972)

In this study, two groups of participants were exposed to loud noise. In the experimental condition, participants were deceived into believing they could control the noise by pressing a button. In the control condition, participants were simply exposed to loud noise. Galvanic skin response (GSR) was used to measure the stress response (arousal levels) of both groups. The experimental group who believed they had control showed lower arousal levels (reduced stress response). It was concluded that people who believe they are in control in stressful situations, even if they actually have no control, are less likely to become stressed.

Langer and Rodin (1976)

In a controlled study, residents in an old people's home were given more personal control over their lives. Those who had choices and who were able to make decisions were more active, happier and lived longer. Those who had no control were less active and less healthy.

Biological psychology: a glossary of terms

biological approaches to stress management: the use of techniques, such as drugs and biofeedback, to change the activity of the body's stress-response system.

cardiovascular disorders: disorders of the heart and blood vessels; for instance, physical damage to the blood-supply system that may in turn lead to the blocking of a blood vessel or vessels.

control: the ability to anticipate events that may happen as well as perceiving that one is able to control the events. The most stressful situations seem to be those in which we feel helpless, believing that nothing we do will change the outcome of events.

general adaptation syndrome: the theory that there are three stages in our response to long-term stress: the alarm stage, in which the sympathetic branch of the autonomic nervous system is activated; the resistance stage, in which the body attempts to cope by maintaining the same level of arousal; and the exhaustion stage, in which the body's resources and defence against the stressor become exhausted.

immune system: a system of cells within the body that is concerned with fighting viruses and bacteria. White blood cells (leucocytes) identify and kill foreign bodies (antigens).

life changes: events (divorce, bereavement, change of job) that cause a person to make a significant adjustment to aspects of their life. These types of life change can be seen as significant sources of stress.

psychological approaches to stress management: the use of techniques such as relaxation or Cognitive Behavioural Therapies (stress inoculation) to help people cope better with stressful situations, or to change the way they perceive the demands of a stressful situation.

stress: a characteristic of the environment, for instance workplace stress, or a situation in which a person perceives they are unable to cope with the demands of what is happening; or the response of the body to a stressful situation.

stress management: the different ways by which people try to cope with the negative effects of stress. They are defined as taking the physical approach, when we try to change the body's response to stress, or as the psychological approach, when we try to change the way we react to a stressful situation.

stressor: an event that causes a stress reaction in the body. Stressors include life events, such as divorce, and workplace stress.

workplace stressor: an aspect of working life, such as work overload or role ambiguity, that we experience as stressful and that causes a stress reaction in our body.

Social psychology: social influence

Social influence

Specification content

- *types of conformity, including internalisation and compliance*
- *explanations of why people conform, including informational social influence and normative social influence*
- *obedience, including Milgram's work and explanations of why people obey*

Social psychology focuses on how we interact with other people and how these interactions may influence our own behaviour. You need to understand how psychologists have defined social influence, psychological explanations of why people yield to majority influence (conformity), and explanations of the processes involved in obedience.

Research into conformity

Conformity as the result of informational social influence (Sherif 1935)

Aim: To measure informational social influence.

Procedures: Participants were shown a still point of light in a dark room. In this situation, an optical illusion called the autokinetic effect occurs, when the point of light appears to move. The participants were asked to estimate how far the point of light had moved, first as individuals, then in a group, and finally as individuals again.

Findings: In the group estimate condition, participants changed their personal estimate and a group norm emerged. This norm was reflected in their final individual estimates.

Conclusion: Since there was no 'factually correct answer', the group norm emerged because individuals looked to others for information.

Conformity as the result of normative social influence (Asch 1956)

Aim: To measure the effect of normative social influence.

Procedures: In a laboratory experiment that used a repeated measures design, groups of seven or eight male students were shown a stimulus line (S) and then three other lines (A, B and C). There was only one 'real' participant in each group. The others were confederates who were helping the experimenter. All the participants were asked to say out loud which line (A, B or C) matched the stimulus line. The real participant always answered last or last but one. Each participant completed 18 trials, and in 12 of the trials (the critical trials), the confederates had all been primed to give the same wrong answer.

Findings: In the control trials, the real participants gave incorrect answers 0.7% of the time. In the critical trials, they gave incorrect answers that conformed to the majority view 37% of the time. Of the real participants, 75% conformed at least once. After the experiment, the real participants were asked why they answered as they had. Some said that they did not believe the answers given by the others in the group but they had not wanted to look different.

Conclusion: Normative social influence had taken place — the real participants agreed with the opinion of the group because they wished to be accepted by them. This demonstrated that participants gave wrong answers because of compliance rather than conversion.

Conformity to social roles (Zimbardo et al. 1973)

Background: There had been a series of violent prison riots in America, and one explanation for this behaviour was that both prisoners and guards have personalities that make conflict inevitable — prisoners lack respect for authority and guards are attracted to the job because of a desire for power. This is a dispositional hypothesis and it suggests that both prisoners and guards are inevitably 'evil'. Zimbardo suggested that it was possible to separate the effects of the prison environment from the personalities of the inhabitants to test the dispositional hypothesis.

Aims: To investigate conformity to social roles and to find out whether conformity is caused by the characteristics of the person (dispositional characteristics), or because of the situation he or she is in (situational factors).

Procedures: An advertisement sought male volunteers, to be paid $15 a day, for a study of 'prison life'. The 24 most stable men (physically and mentally) were selected from 75 volunteers. Participants were randomly assigned to the role of either a prisoner or a guard. There were two reserves and one person dropped out, so in the end there were 10 prisoners and 11 guards, all students, and largely middle-class. A mock prison was built in the basement of Stanford University. It had three small cells equipped with a cot for each prisoner, a solitary confinement cell, various rooms for the guards and an interview room. There was also an indoor 'yard' with an observation screen at one end for video-recording equipment and space for observers.

The prisoners remained in prison throughout the study. The guards worked three-man, 8-hour shifts and were each given a uniform, a whistle, a wooden baton and sunglasses. They were told that they should 'maintain a reasonable degree of order within the prison' but were given no further instructions about how to behave. The prisoners were told to be at home on a particular Sunday. They were 'arrested', booked and fingerprinted and were then blindfolded and driven to the prison. There, they were stripped, deloused and issued with prison uniform: a numbered smock, a light ankle chain, rubber sandals and a cap to make it look as though their hair had been cut off. They were not allowed personal belongings in their cells but were allowed certain 'rights': three meals a day, three supervised toilet trips, 2 hours for reading or letter-writing, and two visiting periods and movies per week. They had to line up three times a day to be counted and tested on the prison rules. The guards only referred to the prisoners by number.

Findings: The prison environment had a huge impact on the feelings and behaviour of all participants. The guards became sadistic and oppressive. They increased the length of the line-ups until some of them lasted several hours. They decided that the prisoners should only receive their rights as a privilege, in return for good behaviour, and some guards volunteered to do extra hours without pay. Punishments included solitary confinement and humiliation. The prisoners, after short-lived resistance, became passive and depressed. Some prisoners coped by becoming sick, whereas others coped by being obedient. Five prisoners had to be released early because of extreme depression (crying, rage and acute anxiety). These symptoms had started to appear within 2 days. The experiment was ended after 6 days, despite the intention to continue for 2 weeks. Even when participants believed they were unobserved, they conformed to their roles.

Conclusions: There was strong evidence of conformity to social roles for prisoners and guards. Afterwards, participants reported that they had 'acted out of character', and there was no lasting change in their private opinions. The conformity was due to the social situation rather than to the personal characteristics of the male student participants. Zimbardo suggested that three processes could explain the prisoners' 'submission':

- **Deindividuation:** the prisoners lost their sense of individuality.
- **Learned helplessness**: the unpredictable decisions of the guards led the prisoners to give up responding.
- **Dependency:** the fact that the prisoners depended on the guards for everything emasculated the men and increased their sense of helplessness.

Evaluation

Sherif (1935)
- **Limitations.** Assessing how far a spot of light has moved is a trivial task and not one that is likely to happen in everyday life. The study has low mundane validity — people may be less likely to be influenced by others in real-life situations.

Asch (1956)
- **Strengths.** The experimental method leads to meaningful results because there is control over variables. Statements can be made about cause and effect. The study can be replicated.
- **Limitations.** The biased sample of male American students may not be representative of other populations. The study has low mundane validity; it does not represent a lifelike social situation. People may not change their opinions about social variables as readily as they do about line lengths. The study was unethical because Asch deceived the participants.

Zimbardo et al. (1973)
- **Strengths.** This research is useful as it can be applied to improve the situation in real prisons, e.g. by training guards to treat prisoners differently.
- **Limitations.** The artificial situation may have led to demand characteristics. The guards and prisoners may have been acting rather than conforming to their roles. It is possible that media stereotypes of aggressiveness may have influenced the guards' behaviour. Thus the study may not have been a valid measure of conformity to social roles. The prisoners and guards were all young and about the same age. A real prison is an established social community and the prisoners do not all arrive at the same time, so the sample did not represent the population of a real prison.

Obedience and conformity: the differences

Obedience
- Obedience occurs within a social hierarchy.
- The emphasis is on social power.
- The obedient behaviour is often different from the behaviour of the authority figure.
- The motivation for behaviour is explicit.
- Participants explain their behaviour in terms of obedience.

Conformity
- Conformity occurs between people of equal status.
- The emphasis is on social acceptance.
- The conformist behaviour is the same as that of the social group.
- The motivation for behaviour is implicit.
- Participants often deny their behaviour is motivated by conformity.

Research into obedience (Milgram 1963)

Milgram points out that obedience can explain some of the worst examples of human behaviour and that it is a commonly observed social fact that 'the individual who is commanded by a legitimate authority ordinarily obeys'.

Aims: Milgram wanted to find out why people obey authority when they are requested to do something unreasonable, what conditions foster obedient behaviour and what conditions foster independent behaviour.

Procedures: Milgram advertised, using a newspaper and direct mailing, for men to take part in a study of memory and learning at Yale University. Everyone was paid $4 for coming to the laboratory and they were told that the payment did not depend on remaining in the study for its duration. The chosen participants were 40 men aged between 20 and 50 who came from various occupational backgrounds.

There were two further participants: the experimenter was a biology teacher, and the learner (Mr Wallace) was a 47-year-old accountant. Both were confederates of Milgram. The participants were deceived about the purpose of the research. They were told that the aim of the experiment was to see how punishment affected learning.

The naïve participant was paired with the confederate and both drew lots to see who would play the part of the 'teacher' and who would be the 'learner'. The confederate always got the part of the learner. The learner was strapped into a chair in the next room attached to an electrode. He was to listen to a list of word pairs and then be given one word and a choice of four possible answers. He was asked to say which of the four was correct. Every time the learner got a question wrong, the teacher would administer an electric shock and the shocks increased in voltage with each mistake. The teacher could see the shock levels displayed on the machine.

The teacher was given a slight shock of 45 volts as a demonstration that the machine was working, but in actuality no other real shocks were given. For the rest of the time, the learner pretended to be receiving shocks. In the experiment, the learner mainly gave wrong answers and for each of these the teacher gave him an electric shock. When the shocks reached 300 volts, the learner pounded on the wall and then gave no response to the next question. When the teacher asked the experimenter for guidance, the experimenter gave the standard instruction, 'an absence of response should be treated as a wrong answer'. After the 315-volt shock, the learner pounded on the wall again but after that, the learner made no other response. If at any time the teacher said he wished to stop, the experimenter used a sequence of four standard 'prods', which were repeated if necessary:

Prod 1: Please continue.
Prod 2: The experiment requires that you continue.
Prod 3: It is absolutely essential that you continue.
Prod 4: You have no other choice, you must go on.

If the teacher asked whether the learner might suffer permanent physical injury, the experimenter said, 'Although the shocks may be painful, there is no permanent tissue damage, so please go on.' If the teacher said that the learner clearly wanted to stop, the experimenter said, 'Whether the learner likes it or not, you must go on until he has learned all the word pairs correctly. So please go on.'

The key findings:
- Twenty-six of the 40 participants (65%) went all the way to 450 volts with the electric shocks.
- Only nine participants (22.5%) stopped at 315 volts.

Other findings: Before the study Milgram had asked 14 psychology students to predict how participants would behave, and the students had estimated that no more than 3% of the participants would continue to 450 volts. People who observed through one-way mirrors were astonished at the participants' behaviour.

The participants showed signs of extreme tension: most of them were observed to 'sweat, tremble, stutter, bite their lips, groan and dig their finger-nails into their flesh', and quite a few laughed nervously.

At the end of the study, all the participants were debriefed. They were reunited with the victim, assured there had been no real shocks and told that their behaviour was normal. They were also sent a follow-up questionnaire which showed that 84% felt glad to have participated, and 74% felt they had learned something of personal importance. Only one person reported that he felt sorry to have participated.

Variations on Milgram's original experiment
The change factors and percentages who obeyed were:
- Experimenter instructed teacher by telephone (distance order); **23%** obedience.
- Experiment moved from Yale to a scruffy office (less prestige in location); **48%** obedience.
- Teacher was in the same room as the learner (increased proximity); **40%** obedience.
- Other teachers refused to give shocks (social support in refusal); **10%** obedience.
- Two teachers, one told by other to give shocks (reduced responsibility); **92.5%** obedience.
- Female participants; **65%** obedience.
- Experimenter was a member of the public (reduced authority); **20%** obedience.

Conclusions
Milgram concluded that ordinary people will obey orders, in conflict with their conscience, even if this means harming someone else, but that situational factors may determine how people will behave:
- **Legitimate authority.** If the person giving the order has legitimate authority, people transfer the responsibility for their actions to the authority figure.
- **Agentic state.** People act as agents of the legitimate authority and hold the authority figure responsible for their actions.
- **The slippery slope.** People follow a small 'reasonable' order and then feel obliged to continue when the orders gradually become unreasonable.

Evaluation

Strengths
- Milgram's experiment increased the understanding of obedience and the dangers of obedience.
- It made obvious the power relationships between authority figures and those they command.
- Most participants said they were glad they had taken part because they learned something of personal importance.
- The participants did believe they were giving shocks (high experimental realism).

Limitations
- There was a lack of informed consent, participants were deceived, and their right to withdraw was breached (though it could be argued that participants could have chosen to leave), which caused stress.
- The sample was biased as they were all male volunteers.
- The task had low external validity because the task did not reflect one that would occur in real life: teachers do not give shocks to students who give wrong answers.
- The experiment may have changed the way participants saw themselves and damaged their self-esteem.

Social influence in everyday life

Specification content

- *explanations of independent behaviour, including how people resist pressures to conform and pressures to obey authority*
- *the influence of individual differences on independent behaviour, including locus of control*
- *implications for social change of research into social influence*

Factors that affect social conformity

Situational and personal variables affect the extent to which people conform.

- **Group size.** The bigger the majority, the more influential it is. In a replication of his original study, Asch tested this and found that with only two confederates, the real participants conformed only 13% of the time. With three confederates, the conformity rate rose to 33%, but increasing the number of confederates to more than three had no effect.
- **Gender.** Some research suggests that females conform more than males, because the norm for female behaviour is to be socially orientated (to want to get on with people). However, Eagly and Carli (1981) suggest that experiments that test conformity use tasks that are more familiar to men. The social norms for female behaviour have also changed in the last two decades.
- **Personality.** Some people are more self-confident and have higher self-esteem than others. Asch suggested that students conformed less than non-students. He proposed that having a high IQ might be associated with lower levels of conformity.
- **Culture.** People raised in collectivist cultures may be more likely to conform than those raised in individualist cultures, because collectivist cultures value interdependence rather than independence. Smith and Bond (1998) found that Belgian students were less likely to conform (by giving wrong answers) than Indian teachers.

Research into obedience in real-life situations

Hofling et al. (1966)

Aim: To study obedience in a real-life setting.

Procedures: Twenty-two nurses working in a hospital were telephoned by an unknown doctor and asked to administer a drug to a patient. The doctor said he would sign the required paperwork later. To obey, the nurses would have to break hospital rules not to take telephone instructions and not to administer drugs unless the paperwork was completed. The dosage instruction was twice the maximum recommended on the drug label.

Findings: Twenty-one nurses obeyed the doctor and would have administered the drug had they not been stopped. The nurses said that they were often given instructions over the telephone and that doctors were annoyed if they refused.

Conclusion: This was a real-life setting in which doctors had high prestige, legitimate authority and power over nurses, and obedience to authority was high.

Meeus and Raaijmakers (1995)

Aim: To study obedience in a real-life setting in Holland.

Procedures: At a time of high unemployment in Holland, 24 participants were asked to conduct interviews to test how 'potential job applicants' responded to stress (the job applicants were in fact trained confederates). The participants were prompted to deliver 15 stressful remarks (e.g. this job is too difficult for you), designed to cause increasing levels of psychological distress. It was assumed that participants would, when they saw the distress they were causing, refuse to continue. The confederates started out by acting in a confident manner but then showed distress and eventually begged the interviewer to stop.

Findings: In spite of seeing the visible distress they were causing, 22 of the 24 participants delivered all 15 stress-causing remarks.

Conclusion: In this realistic face-to-face situation, most participants were obedient and were prepared to cause psychological harm.

Individual differences in obedience or independence

Psychologists propose some predictors of how likely people are to follow orders.

- **Personality.** Adorno suggested that some people have an authoritarian personality, characterised by holding conventional values, being hostile to outgroups, being intolerant to ambiguity and having a submissive attitude to authority. According to Adorno, authoritarian personalities are more likely to obey those in authority.
- **Moral development.** Kohlberg suggested that levels of moral development varied between individuals and that some people reach a level at which their own ethical principles motivate their behaviour. According to Kohlberg, many people operate at a moral level where fear of punishment, or promise of reward, motivate their decisions.

Milgram's findings suggest that people resist authority when:

- the person giving the order is not present or is at a distance (e.g. experimenter instructs teacher by telephone)
- the environment in which the order is given does not have high social prestige (e.g. experiment moved from Yale to a scruffy office)
- there is peer support for disobedience (e.g. other teachers refused to give shocks)
- the person giving the order has no legitimate authority (e.g. experimenter is a member of the public)

Summary of factors affecting obedience or independent behaviour

People are more likely to *resist obedience* if they:
- are self-confident and able to act independently
- have a high level of moral development
- wish to maintain their autonomy and be in control
- have role models who refuse to obey
- are supported by peers who refuse to obey
- are educated as to the dangers of uncritical obedience
- are reminded that they are responsible for the consequences of their actions

The implications of research into social influence for social change

The research by Asch, Milgram and Zimbardo can be used to educate people of the danger of 'blind' obedience to authority.

Zimbardo and Leippe (1991) propose six steps that can be taken to resist pressure to comply, or pressure to obey an authority figure.

(1) Trust your intuition if and when you feel there is 'something wrong'.

(2) Don't just accept the definition of the situation given to you by a person whose interests may conflict with yours.

(3) Consider the 'worst case' scenario (what could happen if you obey?) and act on that possibility.

(4) Figure out an 'escape plan' and act on this as soon as possible.

(5) Don't worry about 'what the other person may think of you' — if you are mistaken, you can always apologise when it is safe to do so.

(6) According to Ross (1988), obedience in Milgram would have been reduced had there been an 'exit button' visible and in easy reach of the participants, who could have pressed it when they wanted to stop.

Think about this 'exit button' idea, and mentally rehearse it as it applies to situations in your life.

Social psychology: a glossary of terms

agentic state: when a person acts as the agent (or tool) of a person having legitimate authority and holds the authority figure responsible for their actions, he or she is in an 'agentic state'.

compliance: conforming to the majority opinion but not agreeing with it. If group pressure is removed, the conformity will cease. Compliance is thought to occur because an individual wishes to be accepted by the majority group.

deindividuation: the loss of a person's sense of individuality. For instance, in the Zimbardo experiment the prisoners and guards lost the sense of 'who they were' in their everyday lives.

identification: conforming to the behaviour expected by the majority, such as obeying school rules about uniform, but without enthusiasm. Identification is thought to occur because an individual wishes to belong to a group.

informational social influence: this occurs when a question asked does not have an obviously correct answer. When this happens, people look to others for information and may agree with the majority view. Informational social influence involves the process of compliance.

internalisation: this occurs when an individual conforms because he or she believes that a group norm for behaviour or a group attitude is 'right'. If group pressure is removed, this conformity will continue.

learned helplessness: the feeling that nothing that one does will change the situation one is in, as in the Zimbardo experiment when the unpredictable decisions of the guards led the prisoners to become passive and depressed.

legitimate authority: when a person giving an order (e.g. a policeman or headteacher) is perceived as having the 'right' to tell others how to behave, they have legitimate authority.

majority influence (conformity): the process that takes place when the views of the dominant group affect an individual's attitudes or behaviour. This may be because of **normative social influence** (the effect of social norms), but can also occur because of **informational social influence** (when the minority yield to group pressure because they think that the majority has more knowledge or information).

minority influence: the process that takes place when a consistent minority changes the attitudes and/or behaviour of an individual. Social psychologists propose that it is the consistency of the minority that is important, since it demonstrates a firm, alternative view to that of the majority. Minority influence leads to a change in attitudes and involves the process of conversion.

normative social influence: this occurs when an individual agrees with the opinions of a group of people because he or she wishes to be accepted by them. The influenced individual may not change his or her private belief.

obedience: a change in behaviour so that people do what a person having authority tells them to do.

social influence: the way that a person or a group of people affect the attitudes and behaviour of another individual.

slippery slope: the course a person takes when he or she follows a small reasonable order, and then feels obliged to continue to obey when the orders gradually become unreasonable.

Individual differences: psychopathology

Defining and explaining psychological abnormality

Specification content

- *definitions of abnormality, including deviation from social norms, failure to function adequately and deviation from ideal mental health, and limitations associated with these definitions of psychological abnormality*
- *key features of the biological approach to psychopathology*
- *key features of the psychological approach to psychopathology, including the psycho-dynamic, behavioural and cognitive approaches*

You must understand and be able to describe how psychologists define abnormality, including statistical infrequency, deviation from social norms, a failure to function adequately and deviation from ideal mental health. You also need to be able to describe and evaluate approaches to psychopathology, including the biological, psychodynamic, behavioural and cognitive approaches.

Definitions of psychological abnormality

Abnormality as behaviour that deviates from the statistical norm

Some psychologists propose that behaviour is normally distributed. If this is true, then people whose behaviour is different (more than two standard deviations above or below the mean) can be defined as 'abnormal'.

> **Evaluation**
>
> - This approach accounts for the frequency of behaviour, not its desirability. A low IQ is, statistically, just as abnormal as a high IQ, but it is desirable to have a high IQ. Therefore, frequency of behaviour tells us nothing about its desirability.
> - It does not allow us to distinguish between rare behaviour that is eccentric (elective), such as keeping snails as pets, and rare behaviour that is psychologically abnormal, such as schizophrenia.
> - It is difficult to define the point at which normal behaviour becomes abnormal behaviour. For example, at what point on the distribution curve does a person's IQ become abnormal?
> - Some behaviour, such as depressive illness, is psychologically abnormal but is not that rare.

Abnormality as behaviour that deviates from the social norm

Some people behave in socially deviant ways. Because their behaviour does not fit in with social norms or meet social expectations, they are seen as different. For example, a person who scavenges in dustbins and hoards rubbish in their home may be seen as abnormal.

Evaluation

- This definition could be used to discriminate against people whom the majority disapprove of and want to remove from society. For example, in the UK in the early part of the twentieth century, unmarried girls who became pregnant could be diagnosed as mentally ill and locked in asylums.
- Whether behaviour is seen as normal depends on its context. Preaching a sermon is seen as normal in a church, but preaching a sermon in a supermarket might be considered abnormal.
- Social norms and attitudes change. Homosexuality was believed to be a mental illness until the 1970s but is not seen as such today.
- Social norms vary within and between cultures; there is not one universally acceptable set of social norms. In Muslim countries, a woman who dressed provocatively in public would be viewed as socially deviant, but this behaviour is common among women in Western society.

Abnormality as failure to function adequately

People who cannot look after themselves or who are perceived to be irrational or out of control are often described as abnormal. The problem with this is that it involves others in making value judgements about what it means to function adequately. The individuals themselves may not think they have a problem and their unusual behaviour may be a way of coping with their difficulties in life.

Abnormality as deviation from ideal mental health

Jahoda (1958) identified six conditions associated with ideal mental health:

(1) a positive self-attitude and high self-esteem
(2) a drive to realise self-potential (personal growth)
(3) the ability to cope with stress
(4) being in control and making your own decisions (personal autonomy)
(5) an accurate perception of reality and the ability to feel for others
(6) the ability to adapt to changes in one's environment

Evaluation

- The degree to which a person meets the six criteria may vary over time. Thus, the degree to which any individual can be defined as 'normal' might vary from day to day.
- It is a subjective standard — it is difficult to measure self-esteem and self-potential.
- It is an ethnocentric standard — it describes normality from an individualistic rather than from a collectivist cultural standpoint.
- By this standard, it is possible that most people could be defined as abnormal.

Cultural relativism in definitions of abnormality

A 'culture' is not a group of people but the customs and attitudes that a group of people share. A 'sub-culture' is a group within a society which shares some practices with the dominant culture but which also has some special attitudes and customs.

Cultural relativism means that we cannot judge normality or abnormality without reference to the norms of the culture where the behaviour arose. Behaviour that may appear abnormal in one cultural setting, because it deviates from the norms of that culture, is not necessarily abnormal in its native cultural setting. Definitions of abnormality are limited because they are culturally specific.

A psychological abnormality can be said to be:
- **Absolute:** if the disorder occurs with the same symptoms and with the same frequency in all cultures. This is probably true for schizophrenia.
- **Universal:** if the disorder occurs in all cultures but not with the same frequency. This is true for some disorders such as depression, which is more common in urban and industrial societies.
- **Culturally relative:** if the disorder is unique (or almost unique) to particular cultures and only meaningful within those cultures. These are called **culture-bound syndromes**.

Because cultures differ in their attitudes and customs, it is not possible to formulate absolute definitions of abnormality. In the Trobriand Islands, it is normal for a son to clean the bones of his dead father and to give them to relatives to wear. It would be seen as abnormal for a widow not to wear the bones of her late husband. In the UK, this behaviour would be seen as abnormal, though in the Victorian age it was quite normal for a widow to wear rings and brooches woven from the hair of her deceased husband.

Approaches to psychopathology

Biological approaches to psychopathology (abnormality) explore differences caused by genetics, biochemistry and brain anatomy. Behavioural approaches look at how the consequences of behaviour reinforce abnormal behaviour and thinking patterns. Psychological approaches to abnormality look at how early childhood experiences, family systems and the unconscious mind affect the way people behave, and how individuals differ in how they think about themselves and the world. Each approach makes different assumptions as to the causes of abnormality.

The biological approach to psychopathology

The biological approach assumes that psychological abnormalities are symptoms of underlying physical causes. Thus, psychological disorders may be referred to as 'mental illnesses'. These are seen as arising from:
- **Genetics.** This is evidenced by the fact that some mental disorders, such as schizophrenia, run in families, suggesting an underlying genetic abnormality. **Evidence for a genetic influence** was found by Kety et al. (1994). In a sample of adoptees with chronic schizophrenia, the prevalence of the disorder was ten times higher

in the biological relatives of the schizophrenic adoptees than in the biological relatives of the control group. This is evidence for the involvement of genetics in schizophrenia. Evidence was also found by Holland et al. (1984). This study of twins showed that where one twin had an eating disorder there was an increased risk of the other twin also having an eating disorder. Holland et al. found a 55% concordance rate for identical twins (MZ twins) compared to 7% for non-identical twins (DZ twins).

- **Infection.** Abnormalities may be caused by infection. General paresis is a condition involving mood swings and delusions and, eventually, paralysis and death. This is caused by syphilis and can now be treated with drugs.
- **Neurotransmitters.** These are biochemicals that carry the signals between brain cells. Too much or too little neurotransmitter may result in psychological disorders. For example, too much dopamine is thought to lead to schizophrenia.
- **Brain injury.** Patients who have suffered a stroke, particularly when the stroke damage is centred in the left hemisphere (in right-handed people), may lose their ability to understand and/or produce speech. Phineas Gage was a construction worker in the 1800s in America. As a result of an explosion, an iron rod penetrated his brain and destroyed part of his frontal lobes. He survived but it was reported that his personality had changed and that he had become disorganised and impulsive.

Evaluation

Strengths
- The biological approach does not blame people for their abnormal behaviour. It has led to a more humane treatment of the mentally ill (better than burning at the stake).
- The scientific status and association with the medical profession means that this approach enjoys credibility.
- Objective evidence shows that biological causes can be linked to psychological symptoms, e.g. dopamine levels in schizophrenia.

Limitations
- Psychiatrists such as Szasz and Laing object to the medical approach. They see the use of labels, such as 'mentally ill', as a way of pathologising people whose behaviour we do not like or cannot explain.
- There may be problems of validity and reliability in diagnosing the type of abnormality. There is frequently a degree of overlap between symptoms of different disorders, meaning the diagnosis may be unreliable.
- The approach takes a reductionist attitude to psychological abnormality and ignores the relationship between the mind and body.

The psychological approaches to psychopathology
The behavioural approach
The behavioural approach makes **three assumptions**. First, it assumes that all behaviour is learned; second, that what has been learned can be unlearned; and third, that abnormal behaviour is learned in the same way as normal behaviour. This model sees the abnormal behaviour as the problem and not a symptom of an underlying cause.

Behaviourists propose that **classical conditioning** can explain phobias. In classical conditioning, an unconditioned stimulus, such as an unexpected loud noise, triggers a natural reflex, e.g. the startle response and fear. But, if another stimulus, e.g. seeing a spider, occurs at the same time, this may in future elicit the fear response. Watson and Rayner (1920) demonstrated how classical conditioning could explain the way in which fear could be learned.

Behaviourists also propose that abnormal behaviour can be learned by the process of **operant conditioning**, in which behaviour is learned through the consequences of our actions. If our actions result in rewarding consequences (positive reinforcement), or in something nasty ceasing (negative reinforcement), we will repeat the behaviour, but we will not repeat behaviour that has bad outcomes. Phobias such as fear of heights can be learned in this way. We become anxious at the thought of climbing the ladder, so we employ a window cleaner in order to avoid using a ladder, and this removes the anxiety (negative reinforcement).

Evaluation

Strengths

- The behavioural approach proposes a simple testable explanation that is supported by experimental evidence.
- The behavioural approach is hopeful as it predicts that people can change (re-learn) their behaviour.

Limitations

- The approach is criticised as being dehumanising and mechanistic (Heather 1976). People are reduced to programmed stimulus–response units.
- The approach cannot explain all psychological disorders. Conditioning cannot cure disorders, e.g. schizophrenia.

The psychodynamic approach

The psychodynamic approach, based on Freudian theory, assumes that behaviour is motivated by unconscious forces, and that abnormal behaviour has its origins in unresolved, unconscious conflicts in early childhood. The model is based on Freud's proposal that the human personality comprises the id, the ego and the superego, and that the development of the personality progresses in five psychosexual stages (the oral, anal, phallic, latent and genital stages). According to the psychodynamic model, in childhood the ego is not fully developed, and is thus unable to manage the conflicting demands of the id and the superego. Conflict and anxiety may result and the ego defends itself by repression, projection or displacement. In repression, anxiety is hidden from the conscious mind (repressed) in the unconscious, but stress in adulthood may trigger the repressed conflict, leading to psychological abnormality.

Evaluation

Strengths

- The psychodynamic approach identifies the importance of traumatic childhood experience in adult problems.

- Freud's theories changed people's attitudes to mental illness; and psychosomatic illnesses demonstrate the link between mind and body.
- The approach does not hold people responsible for their behaviour, as the causes of behaviour are unconscious.

Limitations

- The approach is not scientific: Freud's theories are not falsifiable (his hypotheses are not testable).
- The approach overemphasises past experience, whereas clients' problems may have causes in the 'here and now'.
- The approach is reductionist and ignores biological and socio-cultural factors.

The cognitive approach

The cognitive approach to abnormality is based on the assumption that the human mind is like an information processor and that people can control how they select, store and think about information. The cognitive approach proposes that to be normal is to be able to use cognitive processes to monitor and control our behaviour, and that abnormal behaviour is caused by faulty or irrational thoughts. In the cognitive approach, psychological problems are caused when people make incorrect inferences about themselves or others, and have negative thoughts about themselves and the future. Beck and Clark (1988) found that irrational beliefs were common in patients suffering anxiety and depression. For example, depressive people often believe that they are unloved, that they are failures as parents, and that nothing good will ever happen in the future.

Evaluation

Strengths

- The cognitive approach focuses on how the individual experiences the world and on his or her feelings and beliefs rather than relying on interpretations by other people.
- The approach is hopeful as it assumes people have the power to change their behaviour.

Limitations

- The approach may encourage the idea that people are responsible for their own psychological problems, i.e. that they could be 'normal' if they so chose. This could lead to people being blamed for psychological abnormalities.
- The approach is reductionist, as it ignores biological causes of psychological abnormality such as genetics and biochemistry.

Approaches to psychopathology: a comparison

Four approaches to psychopathology

Approach	Where problems originate	Criticism	Comment
Medical (biological) Abnormality is a symptom of an underlying biological cause: biology of brain, genes etc.	Inside the person. It may be: • inherited/genetic • brain damage • abnormal neuro-transmission	Deterministic. Reductionist. No free will. Can't explain why talking cures or conditioning are effective.	Ignores psychosocial factors but is scientific. Does not 'blame' the individual. Treatment = **drugs/ECT**.
Behavioural Abnormal behaviour is learned and can be unlearned. Abnormal behaviour should be removed/treated.	Abnormal behaviour is learned in inter-action with the environment: • classical or oper-ant conditioning • stimulus–response learning	Deterministic/the past. No free will. Can't explain why drugs or talking cures work.	Ignores biological factors. Does not 'blame' the individual. Treatment based on conditioning (learning).
Psychodynamic Unconscious conflict between id, ego and superego. Behaviour is a symptom of an unseen cause.	Inside the person, during early years: e.g. Oedipus com-plex, repression, regression, ego defences.	Deterministic/the past. No free will. Unscientific, hard to collect empirical evidence. Can't explain why drug treatment is effective.	Ignores biological factors. Does not 'blame' the individual. Treatment = **talking cure, psycho-analysis**.
Cognitive Mental processes not functioning properly.	Inside the person: • irrational thoughts • negative thinking, e.g. depression, 'awfulising'	May 'blame' the individual: if you didn't think irrationally you wouldn't have a problem! Can't explain why drug treatment is effective.	Ignores biological and social factors. Treatment = **talking cure**, CBT.

Treating psychological abnormality

Specification content

- *biological therapies including drugs and ECT*
- *psychological therapies, including psychoanalysis, systematic desensitisation and Cognitive Behavioural Therapy*

You must be able to describe and evaluate treatments based on the biological approach, including drugs and ECT. You must also be able to describe and evaluate psychological therapies, including psychoanalysis, systematic desensitisation and Cognitive Behavioural Therapy.

Treatments based on the biological approach to abnormality

Treatments based on this approach assume that psychological abnormalities are symptoms of some underlying physical cause.

Drug therapies (chemotherapy)

Anti-anxiety (anxiolytic) drugs such as benzodiazepines slow the activity of the central nervous system (CNS), reducing serotonin activity and thus anxiety, and increasing relaxation. Beta blockers act on the autonomic nervous system (ANS) to reduce activity in the ANS associated with anxiety — these drugs reduce heart rate, blood pressure and levels of cortisol. Antipsychotic drugs can be used to reduce mental confusion and delusions. Antidepressant drugs, such as Prozac, can be used to elevate mood. These treatments assume that an imbalance in biochemistry (neurotransmitters) is the cause of the abnormality.

Electroconvulsive therapy (ECT)

ECT is a treatment in which a brief electrical stimulus is given to the brain via electrodes placed on the temples. The electrical charge lasts between 1 and 4 seconds, and causes an epileptic-like seizure. The amount of current needed to induce a seizure (the seizure threshold) can vary up to 40-fold between individuals. Most patients get a total of six to twelve ECTs at a rate of one a day, three times a week. ECT is sometimes given to people with severe depression that has not responded to other forms of treatment such as antidepressants. It is usually only given after the risks have been explained and with the patient's consent. Side effects of ECT can include fear and anxiety, retrograde amnesia and headaches, and Rose et al. (2003) suggested that 33% of patients report long-term memory loss.

Evaluation

Strengths

- It is claimed that biological therapies (drugs) reduce the symptoms of conditions, such as schizophrenia, that could formerly not be treated.
- Drug therapy can be used alongside therapies based on psychological approaches.

- Drug treatments are easy to administer and do not involve the patient changing their lifestyle or behaviour.
- Drug therapies act rapidly to relieve symptoms.

Limitations
- Biological therapies may give rise to ethical concerns. Some drug therapies can have unpleasant side effects. Patients with some conditions may be unable to understand the implications of their treatment and thus be unable to give their informed consent.
- Taking drugs may lead to addiction and dependency.
- Drugs may simply suppress the symptoms, not cure the disorder. The use of drugs may divert attention away from the real causes of the problem.
- Drug treatments take a reductionist approach to the treatment of abnormality because they ignore psychosocial factors.
- No one knows how or why ECT works, and it may cause serious side effects.

Treatments based on the behavioural approach to psychological abnormality

The treatments proposed by the behavioural model are based on the assumption that abnormal behaviour is learned in the same way as normal behaviour and that it can be unlearned. Abnormal behaviour is seen as a 'problem to be cured'.

Behaviourists try to identify the **reinforcers** of abnormal behaviour and change the consequences of behaviour. Behavioural therapies may use:
- **classical conditioning**, in which an undesirable behaviour can be paired with an unpleasant response (aversion therapy)
- **systematic desensitisation**, in which phobics can be gradually reintroduced to a feared object or situation
- **token economies**, based on operant conditioning, are often used in schools and hospitals to change the behaviour of delinquents and anorexics

Behaviour therapy based on operant conditioning
Those behavioural therapies based on operant conditioning assume that behaviour that brings about pleasurable consequences is likely to be repeated, and such therapies are called **behaviour modification**. Behaviour modification can involve positive or negative reinforcement. **Positive reinforcement** means that desired behaviour is rewarded by a pleasant consequence because the use of a reward encourages the likelihood of the behaviour being repeated. For example, if you praise someone for good work you encourage (reinforce) its repetition. **Negative reinforcement** means that desired behaviour is learned because the consequence of the behaviour is that 'something unpleasant' stops happening (or you escape from an aversive stimulus), thus pleasure is felt. Behaviour modification usually involves schedules of reinforcement.

Behaviour modification programmes are used by clinical and educational psychologists to modify the behaviour of children, or adults, with challenging behaviour, and the ABC model is used to explain how behaviour modification programmes work:

A = the antecedent — the trigger (stimulus or event) that elicits the behaviour

B = the behaviour

C = the consequences of the behaviour

Behaviour can be modified by changing either the antecedent or the consequence.

Lovaas et al. (1967) first used operant conditioning in a technique called Applied Behaviour Analysis (ABA), with autistic children who had little or no normal speech. A 'behaviour shaping' technique was used. First, verbal approval is paired with a piece of food (positive reinforcement) whenever the child makes eye contact or pays attention to the therapist's speech. Then the child is reinforced with food or praise whenever any kind of speech sound is made. Once speech sounds occur without prompting, the therapist withholds rewards until the child successfully imitates/utters particular vowels or consonants, then words and finally combinations of words. Many, many reinforcements are needed before the child imitates simple phrases.

Systematic desensitisation

This is a type of behaviour therapy where the undesired behaviour, for instance a person's phobia, is broken down into the small stimulus–response units that comprise it. The therapy consists of:

- the construction of a hierarchy of fears
- training in relaxation — the relaxed state is incompatible with anxiety
- graded exposure (in imagination) and relaxation
- homework — practice in real life

For instance in a phobia of snakes, the least stressful situation might be to look at a picture of a snake and the most stressful might be to have to touch a snake. The therapist works though each S–R unit in the ascending hierarchy, helping the person to replace each dysfunctional response of being afraid, with the response of feeling relaxed. **McGrath et al. (1990)** reported that, following systematic desensitisation, 70% of patients showed improvement in symptoms, but few patients were completely free of anxiety.

Token economy

A token economy is a behaviour modification technique used in psychiatric hospitals, prisons, schools etc. It involves the use of rewards (reinforcement) for desired behaviours that can be exchanged by the recipient for goods, services etc.

Neumark (1998) reports a token economy programme used at Wells Park, a residential school for children aged 7 to 11 with severe emotional or behavioural difficulties (EBD). The token economy system was introduced in 1990 and has been continually refined. Every 5 weeks children, their families and teachers meet to decide and agree the children's 'targets'. Targets might be to 'keep still while I am talking', to 'use a quiet voice' or to 'write in smaller handwriting'. Every 15 minutes from Monday to Friday each child has an opportunity to receive a token; and every day at 3.45 p.m. the children can 'cash in' tokens in groups of five, called 'giants', for treats such as books, toys or extra play. More ambitious children can save up 'giants' for shopping trips or outings. The token economy is effective because all the teachers operate the system in the same way; children previously described as unteachable or hyperactive sit down, read and enjoy learning, and can increase their reading age by 2 or 3 years in the first year at the school.

Evaluation

Strengths
- Behavioural therapies are effective for treating phobias, obsessive compulsive disorders and eating disorders, and are appropriate for those whose symptoms are behavioural.
- The behavioural model is hopeful as it predicts that people can change (re-learn) their behaviour.

Limitations
- Token economies involving reinforcers that withhold a basic human right, such as food, clothing or privacy, are unethical and such procedures have been ruled illegal in the USA.
- These therapies are only effective for a limited number of disorders. Conditioning cannot cure all disorders, e.g. schizophrenia.

Treatments based on the psychodynamic approach to psychological abnormality

These treatments are based on the assumption that abnormal behaviour is motivated by unconscious forces. Treatments are focused on three objectives: first, to free healthy impulses; second, to strengthen and re-educate the ego; and third, to change the superego so that it causes less anxiety. This is achieved by **psychoanalysis**, during which dream analysis and free association may be used. In **free association**, the therapist interprets pauses or hesitations when talking about certain topics as signs of repressed anxiety; this is based on the idea that the ego will try to repress unacceptable impulses. In **dream analysis**, the therapist interprets dreams as symbols of repressed wishes; this is based on Freud's proposal that dreams represent unconscious wish-fulfilment. In **thematic apperception tests**, the client may reveal unconscious thoughts, which the therapist interprets. In the process of **transference**, the client transfers repressed conflicts onto the therapist, who 'becomes the parent' that the child lacked or needed to resolve the unconscious conflict.

Evaluation

Strength
- Freud's theories changed people's attitudes to mental illness, and psychotherapy has been found to be effective in psychosomatic illnesses.

Limitations
- Eysenck (1952) found that 66% of patients in therapy recover within 2 years, but so do 66% of patients who have no therapy.

- Psychoanalysis may only benefit certain clients — the young, attractive, verbal, intelligent and successful (the YAVIS model) — and is more likely to be effective with clients who have a positive attitude (belief) towards therapy (a self-fulfilling prophecy).
- The treatment takes a long time and is expensive.

Treatments based on the cognitive approach to psychological abnormality

Treatments based on this model focus on helping the patient to change irrational or negative thoughts to ones that are rational and positive. The objective of treatment is to correct unrealistic ideas through cognitive restructuring, so that thinking becomes an effective means of controlling behaviour. The therapist supports the patient through a process of Cognitive Behaviour Therapy (CBT) until thought processes become more rational. Examples of treatments based on the cognitive model are rational emotive therapy for depression (Beck 1976) and stress inoculation training (Meichenbaum).

Rational emotive behaviour therapy (REBT)

Ellis (1975) developed rational emotive therapy (RET) based on the idea that some people have persistent self-defeating thoughts that are irrational. According to Ellis, irrational beliefs that may cause needless upset can be identified when we catch ourselves thinking 'should' or 'must' in ways that are subjective and judgemental. Thoughts such as 'I **must** be approved of by everybody' or 'I **should** always achieve in everything I do' are irrational; and believing these, or similar, irrational statements is self-defeating because this way of thinking prevents us from taking constructive action to change ourselves, or to change the situation. REBT aims to challenge this way of thinking by helping clients to recognise their irrationality and the consequences of their habitual way of thinking. In REBT clients are taught to recognise and replace their 'irrational' thoughts with more constructive and realistic ones. As with behaviour modification, an ABC model can be used to explain what happens.

A We experience an **activating event** leading to emotional arousal (e.g. receiving a poor grade in an exam).

B A **belief** is developed about the event that may be rational (e.g. I would have done better had I revised more effectively) or irrational (e.g. I must be thick and don't deserve to do better).

C Behavioural **consequences** ensue from our beliefs, which may be productive (e.g. deciding to re-sit the exam and revising hard) or unproductive (e.g. dropping out of class).

In REBT a person is encouraged to realise that it is not the 'events in themselves' that lead to negative consequences but the self-defeating beliefs that we develop about the events. Clients are encouraged to change the way they think about events in their lives by:

- **logical disputing**: asking themselves whether the way they think 'makes sense'
- **empirical disputing**: asking themselves whether there is proof that their belief is accurate

- **pragmatic disputing**: asking themselves whether the way they think is helpful to them

Effective internal disputation changes self-defeating beliefs into more rational beliefs that help the client feel better about him- or herself.

Evaluation

Strengths
- Cognitive therapy focuses on how the individual experiences the world and on his or her feelings and beliefs, rather than relying on interpretations by other people.
- Cognitive-based therapies may increase self-efficacy and self-belief and thus improve people's lives in the future.
- Supporting evidence from Hollon et al. (1992) found that CBT was more effective than drugs for treating depression and anxiety.

Limitations
- Treatments may only be effective for people who have good problem-solving skills, an insight into their behaviour and the willingness to spend time on 'the problem'.
- Treatments may only be effective for anxiety disorders and depressive illnesses. They may not be generalisable to many psychological abnormalities.

Psychopathology: a glossary of terms

abnormality: a psychological condition, or behaviour, that differs from how most people behave and that is harmful, or which causes distress to the individual or those around them. Abnormal behaviour is behaviour that does not match society's idea of what is appropriate.

behavioural approach to abnormality: an approach that sees the abnormal behaviour as the problem rather than as the symptom of an underlying cause. It makes three assumptions: first, that all behaviour is learned; second, that what has been learned can be unlearned; and third, that abnormal behaviour is learned in the same way as normal behaviour.

biological approach to abnormality: an approach that assumes that psychological abnormalities are symptoms of underlying physical causes.

classical conditioning: treatment, based on the behavioural approach, in which an undesirable behaviour can be paired with an unpleasant response (aversion therapy).

cognitive approach to abnormality: an approach that proposes that to be normal is to be able to use cognitive processes to monitor and control our behaviour. By this view, abnormal behaviour is caused by faulty or irrational thoughts, or when people make incorrect inferences about themselves or others, and/or about themselves and the future.

cultural relativism: the view that behaviour can only be judged properly in the context of the culture in which it originates.

deviation from ideal mental heath: abnormality is seen as a deviation from an ideal of positive mental health, when ideal mental health includes having a positive attitude towards oneself, resistance to stress and an accurate perception of reality.

deviation from social norms: abnormal behaviour is seen as a deviation from the implicit rules about how one 'ought' to behave, where any behaviour that does not 'fit in' with these social rules is considered to be abnormal.

drug therapy: treatment based on the biological approach, which assumes that an imbalance in biochemistry (neurotransmitters) is the cause of the abnormality. Drug treatments may include anti-anxiety drugs, such as benzodiazepines, to slow the activity of the central nervous system (CNS), reducing serotonin activity and thus anxiety. Antipsychotic drugs can be used to reduce mental confusion and delusions. Antidepressant drugs, such as Prozac, can be used to elevate mood.

electroconvulsive therapy (ECT): a treatment in which a brief electrical stimulus is given to the brain via electrodes placed on the temples. The electrical charge lasts between 1 and 4 seconds, and causes an epileptic-like seizure. ECT is sometimes given to people with severe depression that has not responded to other forms of treatment such as antidepressants.

failure to function adequately: if behaviour interferes with how people function in their everyday lives, for instance being unable to care for themselves, the behaviour is seen as abnormal.

psychodynamic approach to abnormality: the assumption that behaviour is motivated by unconscious forces, and that abnormal behaviour has its origins in unresolved, unconscious conflicts in early childhood. This approach (based on Freud's theories) suggests that the ego defends itself by repression, projection or displacement. In repression, anxiety is hidden from the conscious mind (repressed) in the unconscious, but stress in adulthood may trigger the repressed conflict, leading to psychological abnormality.

rational emotive behaviour therapy (REBT): a treatment, based on the cognitive approach to abnormality, in which clients are taught to recognise and replace their 'irrational' thoughts with more constructive and realistic ones.

statistical infrequency: abnormality is defined as any behaviour that is rare.

systematic desensitisation: treatment based on the behavioural approach in which a person having a phobia can be gradually reintroduced to a feared object or situation.

token economy: treatment based on the behavioural approach; it is a behaviour modification technique used in psychiatric hospitals, prisons, schools etc. and involves the use of rewards (reinforcement) for desired behaviour that can be exchanged by the recipient for goods, services etc.

Questions
&
Answers

In this section there are 13 questions — four on biological psychology, five on social psychology and four on individual differences.

The section is structured as follows:
- sample questions in the style of the Unit 2 exam
- examples of candidate responses equivalent to B/C/D-grade level (candidate A) demonstrating strengths and weaknesses and the potential for improvement
- examples of candidate responses equivalent to A-grade level (candidate B) demonstrating a thorough knowledge, a good understanding and an ability to deal with the data presented in the question

Examiner comments

All candidate responses are followed by examiner comments. These are preceded by the icon 𝑒. Examiner comments may indicate where credit is due, strengths in the answer, areas for improvement, specific problems, common errors, lack of clarity, irrelevance, mistakes in meanings of terms and/or misinterpretation of the question.

Comments may also indicate how example answers *might be marked* in an exam, using the mark allocations listed on pages 7–8.

Note: because the first examination of this unit is in January 2009, students and teachers should remember that this unit guide is published before any candidates have actually taken an exam. Thus all examiner comments are based on the marking guidelines as published by AQA.

Biological psychology (1)

Outline the effect that stress may have on the immune system. (6 marks)

Question injunction = outline. This question requires you to show **AO1 skills.**You need to demonstrate your understanding of how stress affects the immune system.You are not expected to provide more than 5–6 minutes of writing. There are several ways to approach this question.You could focus on:

- *the process by which stress affects the immune system,* by referring to the immunosuppressive effect of stress, in which there is a reduction of the ability to deal with antigens and a decrease in the production of T cells that attack cells infected with viruses
- *the outcomes of the effect of stress on the immune system,* where an example of this is evidence by Kiecolt-Glaser on the effect of chronic stress on wound healing

You could use a mixture of both approaches, and first focus on the process and then give evidence for the outcome of the effect of stress.

■ ■ ■

Answers

Candidate A

Kiecolt-Glaser aimed to establish a link between stress and reduced immune system. They looked for evidence of a difference in immune response to stress and whether factors such as anxiety were associated with immune system functioning. A sample of first-year medical students volunteered to give blood samples one month before their final exams and after their exams. The blood samples were analysed for how much 'natural killer cell' activity was present. In the blood sample after the exams, natural killer cell activity was significantly reduced and was most reduced in students who were experiencing other stressful events. This study shows that stress has an immunosuppressant effect.

Candidate B

The immune system consists of cells in the bloodstream, most notably white blood cells that defend the body against bacteria and viruses. Stress directly reduces the ability of the immune system to protect us against antigens, which leads to an increased likelihood of physical illness. This is because of the immunosuppressive effect of stress in which there is a reduction of the ability to deal with antigens and a decrease in the production of T cells that attack cells infected with viruses. In long-term stress increased levels of corticosteroids reduce the production of antibodies leaving the body more susceptible to disease.

Both answers provide accurate information.

Candidate A takes an 'evidence'-based approach to the question, and gives an accurate and reasonably detailed outline of appropriate evidence of the effect of stress on the immune system. There is appropriate selection of evidence to demonstrate knowledge and understanding. This answer would probably be awarded 4–5 marks.

Candidate B takes a process-based approach to the question, and gives an accurate and reasonably detailed outline of the process by which stress affects the immune system that demonstrates sound knowledge and understanding. This answer would probably be awarded 5–6 marks.

Biological psychology (2)

Outline the use of drugs in the control of stress. (4 marks)

🖉 **Question injunction = outline.** This question requires you to show **AO1 skills**. You need to demonstrate your understanding of how drugs are used to control stress by writing a brief outline of the use of two or more drugs. You are not expected to provide more than 4–5 minutes of writing. You should briefly state what effect the drugs have and then elaborate how the drugs work. You could include:

- Drugs are used as a direct treatment to reduce the biological symptoms of stress.
- Drugs are fast acting and easy to use.
- Anxiolytic drugs/tranquillisers are used to treat stress symptoms.
- Benzodiazepines act on neurotransmitters to cause relaxation and reduce anxiety.
- Beta blockers act on the sympathetic nervous system to reduce blood pressure and heart rate.

Although the question asks about the 'use of drugs' you might be able to gain 4 marks if you focus on the effect(s) of one drug in detail.

■ ■ ■

Answers

Candidate A

Drugs such as anxiolytics are used as a direct treatment to reduce the biological symptoms of stress. The advantage of drug treatment is that drugs are fast acting and easy to use. However a disadvantage is that drugs may cause side effects.

Candidate B

Drugs are used as a direct treatment to reduce the biological symptoms of stress and are fast acting and easy to use. Benzodiazepine anti-anxiety drugs such as Valium work by reducing the activity of the neurotransmitter serotonin causing relaxation and reduced anxiety. Beta blockers reduce the activity in the sympathetic nervous system to reduce heart rate and blood pressure, preventing the development of cardio-vascular disorders.

🖉 There is a clear difference in the quality of these answers.

Candidate A gives an accurate but brief outline of an appropriate drug treatment in the first sentence, and credit would be given for the accuracy of the answer. However, the candidate then wastes time by writing an evaluative comment that was not required by the question. This answer would probably be awarded 1–2 marks.

Candidate B provides an accurate and detailed outline of why drugs are used, and then elaborates to accurately identify some specific drug treatments and how more than one type of drug work. The strength of the answer is that by appropriate selection of material the candidate demonstrates clear knowledge and understanding, and the answer would probably be awarded 4 marks.

Biological psychology (3)

Discuss the view that stress is environmentally determined. (12 marks)

✏ **Question injunction = discuss.** This question assesses **AO1 and AO2 skills**.

AO1 = 6 marks for a description of environmental determinants (causes) of stress

AO2 = 6 marks for commentary and evaluation

To gain AO1 marks you should briefly describe research into environmental stressors, either one study in detail or more than one study in less detail. You could describe:

- research by Holmes and Rahe into the effect of life changes
- research by DeLongis into the effect of daily hassles
- research into stress caused by work-related factors such as lack of control or work overload

To gain AO2 marks you could focus on the strengths and weaknesses of the research you described by evaluating the findings and implications and/or commenting on methodological issues arising from the quoted research. You could also comment on alternative views, such as the effect of personality factors (Friedman and Rosenman — Type A personality; and/or Kobasa — hardiness) and/or contradictory evidence. For high marks you need to express your ideas clearly, using appropriate psychological terminology, to demonstrate a clear understanding. You can address either a broad range of issues in reasonable depth or a narrower range of issues in greater depth. Make sure you focus on *the view that stress is environmentally determined*.

For this split AO1 /AO2 question you should write a quick plan before you write your answer. You need to provide about 6–7 minutes of content for the AO1 section and 6–7 minutes of content for the AO2 section. Do not waste time writing 'all you know about stress' — your answer should provide as much AO2 content as AO1 content.

■ ■ ■

Answers

Candidate A

Holmes and Rahe constructed the social readjustment rating scale (SRRS), which is a questionnaire on which participants tick the life events they have experienced in the last 12 months, giving a measure of the amount of life change (stress) a person has experienced. Holmes and Rahe found that a person having 300 life change points over 12 months had an 80% chance of becoming ill — perhaps because when people are required to change their lifestyle they get stressed. DeLongis created a hassles scale to assess the effect of everyday problems of life, such as getting stuck in a traffic jam. The hassles scale measures positive events (uplifts) as well as hassles. They found that the hassles scale was a better predictor of ill health than the SRRS and concluded that people who experience more hassles than uplifts may be at increased risk of stress-related illness.

Both these studies provided a measure of the relationship between environmental factors such as hassles and life changes, and stress. However, the subjective experience of a life event is different for each person. Also, because the research is correlational, we cannot say that life changes cause stress, only that these factors may be related. Individual differences can also determine whether people suffer stress. Friedman and Rosenman describe the Type A personality as having a behaviour pattern that is time-pressured which increases the individual's experience of stress. This suggests that stress is caused by a combination of individual characteristics as well as environmental factors.

Candidate B

Psychologists have researched environmental determinants such as life changes, daily hassles and factors in the workplace. Holmes and Rahe constructed the social readjustment rating scale (SRRS) to correlate the amount of life change people had experienced (stress) with their physical illnesses. The SRRS is a questionnaire on which participants tick the life events they have experienced in the last 12 months, giving a measure of the amount of life change (stress) a person has experienced. Holmes and Rahe found that a person having 300 life change points over 12 months had an 80% chance of becoming ill. This suggests that environmental changes, such as changes in lifestyle, can be the cause of stress.

However, the subjective experience of a life event is different for each person and an event that may be stressful for one may have little effect on another.

An alternative approach was taken by DeLongis, who pointed out that a life change event, such as marriage or divorce, happens infrequently. DeLongis created a hassles scale to assess the effect of everyday problems of life, such as getting stuck in a traffic jam. The hassles scale measured positive events (uplifts) as well as hassles. They found that the hassles scale was a better predictor of ill health than the SRRS and concluded that people who experience more hassles than uplifts may be at increased risk of stress-related illness. This research also supports the suggestion that environmental factors are a cause of stress. However, because both the Holmes & Rahe and DeLongis research is correlational, we cannot say that life changes, or hassles, determine stress, only that these two factors may be related.

Psychologists have also researched whether the work environment causes stress. Johnson and Hall investigated the relationship between workplace stressors and cardiovascular disease. Participants answered questions about the amount of control they had and their social relationships at work. One of the findings was that demanding jobs involving low levels of control were related to increased incidence of heart disease, which supports the view that environmental factors cause stress. This research was useful because it showed how factors such as control are important in understanding workplace stress. However, self-report methods may result in inaccurate descriptions of job characteristics and may be biased by personality characteristics, both of which may lead to unreliable results. Also, it is possible that the association found between job stress and illness is caused by other factors. For example, workers on the shop floor may experience a lack of control and noisy work environments and are also more likely to have poorer living conditions because of

lower wages. Also, jobs that are perceived as stressful by some will be enjoyed by others. Friedman and Rosenman describe the Type A personality as having a behaviour pattern that is time-pressured, competitive and hostile, which increases the individual's experience of stress. This suggests that stress is caused by individual characteristics as well as environmental factors.

Both answers provide accurate information.

Candidate A provides accurate and reasonably detailed evidence suggesting that environmental factors cause stress and demonstrates knowledge and understanding. There is evidence of selection of appropriate material to address the question as to why life changes and hassles may cause stress. The candidate then evaluates a restricted range of issues appropriate to the evidence quoted, but each issue is reasonably clearly explained. A strength of the evaluation is the use of the Friedman and Rosenman evidence to point out that stress is likely to be caused by interaction between individual differences and environmental factors. The answer would probably be awarded 4 + 3/4 marks.

Candidate B leaves nothing to chance. The answer provides an accurate and detailed account of a wide range of evidence suggesting that environmental factors cause stress and demonstrates sound knowledge and understanding. There is evidence of selection of appropriate material to address the question as to why life changes, hassles and work-related factors may determine stress. The candidate evaluates a wide range of issues appropriate to the evidence quoted and each issue is clearly explained. One strength of the evaluation is the comparison of the Holmes and Rahe with the DeLongis research and the coherence of the arguments in pointing out that stress is likely to be caused by interaction between environmental factors and individual differences; another strength is the balance of AO1 and AO2 content. The answer would probably be awarded 6 + 6 marks. However, this answer is about 480 words, which is probably longer than most candidates would manage to write in 15 minutes.

Biological psychology (4)

Evaluate the use of psychological treatments to manage the negative effects of stress. (6 marks)

🖉 **Question injunction = evaluate.** This question assesses **AO2 skills**. To gain AO2 marks you could focus on the strengths and weaknesses of the use of psychological treatments to manage the negative effects of stress. You could also comment on the assumptions of psychological approaches to stress and alternatives to psychological treatments. For high marks you need to express your ideas clearly, using appropriate psychological terminology to demonstrate a clear understanding. You can address either a broad range of issues in reasonable depth or a narrower range of issues in greater depth.

You need to provide about 6–7 minutes of content for the AO2 section. Do not waste time describing 'all you know about psychological treatment' — your answer should be an evaluation!

■ ■ ■

Answers

Candidate A

Psychological treatments such as stress inoculation (Meichenbaum) focus on helping people cope better in stressful situations, but these treatments may not be effective in anxious people; drug treatments, such as anxiolytics, may be more effective in the first instance. Also, psychological treatments may only be successful with patients who are able to take the time and make the effort to help themselves, thus psychological treatment may not be generalisable. Also, compared to drugs, there are no side effects to psychological treatments.

Candidate B

Psychological treatments focus on the *cause* of stress rather than the symptoms, which means that if the treatment is effective, the cause of stress is removed. The treatments are effective for both short and long-term stress and can be effectively combined with drug treatment. However, treatments such as stress inoculation (Meichenbaum) and hardiness training (Kobasa) focus on helping people cope better in stressful situations, but they do not immediately relieve the biological effects of stress. As such, psychological treatments may not be effective in anxious people; drug treatments, such as anxiolytics, may be more effective in the first instance. Also, psychological treatments may only be successful with patients who are able to take the time and make the effort to help themselves, and research findings are often based on a narrow sample, mainly white, middle-class, educated people, thus psychological treatment may not be effective with other populations.

question

However, psychological treatments not only reduce stress, but increase self-confidence and self-efficacy, making it more likely that the person will be able to deal with stress in the future. Also, there are no biological side effects and once the course of treatment is paid for, future self-administered treatment is free.

🖉 There is a clear difference in the quality of these answers.

Candidate A provides an accurate but basic evaluation of a narrow range of issues. The answer starts off well but the final two issues are not fully explained/elaborated. The answer would probably be awarded 2–3 marks.

Candidate B provides an accurate and detailed evaluation. The strength of this answer is that the candidate starts by demonstrating a good understanding of psychological treatment for stress. The candidate uses a good range of specialist terms to discuss a wide range of appropriate issues and each issue is clearly explained. The strength of this evaluation is the coherence of the argument and the balance between the advantages and limitations of psychological treatments for stress. The answer would probably be awarded 5–6 marks.

Question 5

Social psychology (1)

Outline what is meant by normative social influence. (4 marks)

Question injunction = outline. This question requires you to show **AO1 skills**. You need to demonstrate that you know and understand what is meant by *normative* social influence. You are not required to give evidence and do not need to provide more than 4 minutes of writing.

■ ■ ■

Answers

Candidate A

Social influence is the way that a person or a group of people can affect the attitudes and behaviour of another individual to make them agree with them.

Candidate B

Social influence is the way a person or a group of people can affect the attitudes and behaviour of another individual, and normative social influence occurs when an individual agrees with the opinions of a group of people because he or she wishes to be accepted by them. In normative social influence the influenced individual may not change his or her private belief.

There is a clear difference in the quality of these answers.

Candidate A has either not read the question carefully, or does not know what is meant by normative social influence. This answer would probably be awarded 0–1 marks.

Candidate B provides an accurate and detailed outline of normative social influence, demonstrating a sound understanding. The strength of this answer is in the accurate use of psychological terminology. This answer would probably be awarded 4 marks.

Social psychology (2)

Explain the difference between normative and informational social influence. (3 marks)

Question injunction = explain. This question requires you to show **AO2 skills**. You need to demonstrate your understanding by writing a detailed and accurate explanation of the difference between normative and informational social influence.

There are three differences and marks will probably be awarded for identification of each difference or a detailed explanation of one difference. Differences include:

- the need to be accepted by others versus the need for accurate information from others
- the use of others as a model for acceptable behaviour versus the use of others as a source of information
- the internalisation of belief versus compliance

You are not expected to provide more than about 3 minutes of writing. In your answer you should first identify the difference(s) and then explain the implications of the difference(s).

■ ■ ■

Answers

Candidate A
Normative social influence occurs when an individual agrees with the opinions of a group of people because he or she wishes to be accepted by them. Informational social influence occurs when a person looks to others for information, perhaps because a question does not have a 'right' answer, and then agrees with the opinion of the group.

Candidate B
Normative social influence occurs when an individual agrees with the opinions of a group of people because he or she wishes to be accepted by them, but the influenced individual may not change his or her private belief. Thus normative social influence does not involve the process of compliance. This is different to the process of informational social influence, which occurs when a person looks to others for information and then agrees with the majority view, which does involve the process of compliance.

There is a clear difference in the quality of these answers.

> **Candidate A** has briefly outlined a definition of normative and informational social influence but has ignored the question injunction to explain the difference; thus the content of the answer is AO1, and while the answer is accurate it is little more than a statement. The answer would probably be awarded 1 mark.

Candidate B provides an accurate and detailed explanation demonstrating an understanding of the difference between normative and informational influence. The strength of this answer is that the candidate uses psychological terminology accurately to demonstrate that he/she has a sound understanding of the process involved in both normative and informational social influence. The answer would probably be awarded 3 marks.

Social psychology (3)

Explain how psychological research helps us to understand why people are influenced by others.

(6 marks)

✍ **Question injunction = explain.** This question assesses your **AO2 skills.** You need to demonstrate your understanding of one or more studies of social influence and the implications and applications of the research findings.

You could focus on the following research:
- the Milgram study in why people obey orders from a legitimate authority
- the Asch study in conformity
- the Zimbardo prison experiment
- the Hofling field experiment in obedience in nurses

One mark will probably be awarded for an accurate but brief outline of research, and further marks will be awarded for explanation as to how this research helps us understand social influence. You are not expected to provide more than about 6 minutes of writing. Don't forget to focus on the question injunction 'explain'.

■ ■ ■

Answers

Candidate A

At Yale university, Milgram conducted a laboratory experiment into obedience and found that 26 of 40 male participants administered a 450-volt electric shock. This suggests that people are influenced to obey orders because the person giving the order has legitimate authority, and that they transfer the responsibility for their actions to the authority figure and/or they act as agents of the legitimate authority and do not take responsibility for their own actions.

Candidate B

In the original study at the University of Yale, when the context in which the order was given was one of prestige and high social status, 26 of 40 participants administered a 450-volt electric shock. This suggests that people are influenced to obey orders when the person giving the order has legitimate authority, because they transfer the responsibility for their actions to the authority figure and/or they act as agents of the legitimate authority, holding the authority figure responsible for their actions. Milgram also helps us to understand the 'slippery slope argument' that people may follow a small 'reasonable' order and then feel obliged to continue when the orders gradually become unreasonable. Milgram also explains factors that encourage independence, for example Milgram found that when the order to continue giving shocks was given from a distance (over the telephone), participants were less likely to obey and also that when others present refused to continue, participants were less likely to obey. This suggests that orders given 'face to face' have more influence and that disobedience is increased by social support. In another study of social influence, the Zimbardo prison experiment, male students who were randomly allocated the role of prison guard became oppressive and treated the prisoners badly, which explains why people who are given social power may abuse their power and behave in an oppressive manner.

Both candidates provide reasonable answers though candidate B has provided a more extensive answer.

Candidate A has selected appropriate material and has given an accurate explanation of how this research helps us to understand why people obey others. The weakness of this answer is that the candidate focuses on a limited range of research and explanations of social influence. The answer would probably be awarded 3 marks.

Candidate B also focuses mainly on the Milgram research and effectively selects material to elaborate accurately a wide range of explanations of what this research tells us about social influence. The candidate provides detailed explanations demonstrating a sound knowledge and understanding. The strength of this answer is that the candidate uses psychological terminology accurately to demonstrate that he/she has a good appreciation of how our understanding of social influence has been increased by psychological research. The answer would probably be awarded 5–6 marks.

Social psychology (4)

Discuss one ethical issue raised by the Milgram research. (4 marks)

e **Question injunction = discuss.** Because the question is focused on the ethics of research the question assesses your **AO3 skills.** You need to demonstrate your understanding of one of the ethical issues arising from the Milgram research and why these ethical issues arose. You could discuss problems such as *gaining informed consent* and/or giving participants *the right to withdraw* when studying obedience and/or the problems of deciding whether breaking the ethical guidelines can be justified by what we have learned.

Ethical issues arising from the Milgram study include:
- deception and thus prevention of fully informed consent
- psychological harm to the participants caused by the stress of the situation
- the perception of participants that they were unable to withdraw

■ ■ ■

Answers

Candidate A

Psychologists are supposed to gain fully informed consent from their participants and this means that participants should not be deceived about what they will be asked to do. Milgram broke this ethical guideline because participants were deceived. They were told that the learner was another participant but he was a stooge, and they were led to believe that the electric shocks were real but the learner was only pretending.

Candidate B

Psychologists should gain fully informed consent from their participants and this means that participants should not be deceived about what they will be asked to do. Milgram broke this ethical guideline because participants were deceived, for example, they were led to believe that the electric shocks were real but the learner was only pretending. In ethical research, participants are given the right to withdraw, but Milgram's participants were prodded to remain even though they were trembling with stress. However, at the end of the study, Milgram thoroughly debriefed his participants, who said they were happy to have taken part. This research taught us a lot about why ordinary people can be influenced to obey immoral orders, but if Milgram had told his participants the truth about the experiment he could not have measured obedience.

e There is a clear difference in the quality of these answers.

Candidate A has identified an appropriate ethical issue arising from the Milgram research, but the answer is more descriptive than explanatory. This is a common error. To improve this answer the candidate could have explained the problems involved in the study of obedience, such as the problem of giving the right to withdraw, and/or how to assess the value of research against the right of participants. The answer would probably be awarded 2 marks.

Candidate B accurately identifies more than one ethical issue arising from the Milgram research, and through effective use of material elaborates the ethical issues. The candidate demonstrates sound knowledge and understanding, by providing an argument to defend Milgram (the debriefing of participants) and an explanation of the value of the research. The strength of this answer is that the candidate uses psychological terminology accurately to demonstrate a sound understanding of the ethical issues arising in Milgram and of the problems that arise in resolving these issues. The answer would probably be awarded 4 marks.

Social psychology (5)

Describe and evaluate research into social influence. (12 marks)

 Question injunction = describe and evaluate. This question assesses **both AO1 and AO2 skills**, with 6 marks awarded for AO1 skills and 6 marks awarded for AO2 skills.

For the 'describe' (AO1) part of the question, you should briefly describe research into social influence. There is a wide range of studies that can be included, such as:

- Asch: research into normative social influence
- Sherif: research into informational social influence
- Milgram: study of obedience
- Zimbardo: study into conformity to social roles
- Hofling: study of obedience

For the 'evaluate' (AO2) part of the question, you might focus on the strengths and weaknesses of the research methods used in the research you have outlined, and/or evaluate the findings and implications. For high marks you need to express your ideas clearly, using appropriate psychological terminology, to demonstrate a clear under-standing. You can address either a broad range of issues in reasonable depth or a narrower range of issues in greater depth. Make sure you focus on the question of research into social influence.

For this split AO1 /AO2 question you should write a quick plan before you write your answer. You need to provide about 6 minutes of content for the AO1 section and 6 minutes of content for the AO2 section. Do not waste time writing 'all you know about research into social influence' — your answer should provide as much AO2 content as AO1 content.

■ ■ ■

Answers

Candidate A: AO1 section

Asch did a laboratory experiment to study conformity. Students were shown a stimulus line and then three other lines. There was only one 'real' participant in each group. All the participants were asked to say out loud which of the three lines matched the stimulus line. The real participant always answered last or last but one and gave incorrect answers that conformed to the majority view 37% of the time, and 75% conformed at least once. After the experiment, the real participants were asked why they answered as they had and some said they had not wanted to look different.

Zimbardo set up a mock prison to see how the situation influenced behaviour. The prison cells had bars like real prisons and the guards wore military-style uniforms and carried sticks. Male students were allocated to the role of either prisoner or guard, and the guards became sadistic and oppressive and their punishments included solitary confinement and humiliation. The prisoners became passive and depressed. Zimbardo concluded that the behaviour was due to the situation rather than to the personal characteristics of the participants.

Candidate A: AO2 section

The advantage of using a laboratory experiment is that there is control over variables so statements can be made about cause and effect. But the biased sample of male students may not be representative of other populations. Also the Asch study was unethical because he deceived the participants.

The strength of the Zimbardo research is that it is useful, as it can be applied to improve the situation in real prisons, by training guards to treat prisoners differently. The weakness is that the guards and prisoners may have been acting. Also, the participants were all young students so the findings can't be generalised to a real prison.

Candidate B: AO1 section

Many psychologists have researched social influence. Sherif aimed to investigate informational social influence and found that the formation of social norms can result when people are asked questions about an ambiguous stimulus. In this study the movement of the spot of light was an illusion but a group norm emerged because individuals looked to others for information. In another study of social influence, Asch conducted a laboratory experiment into normative social influence, and found that student participants gave wrong answers, agreeing with the opinion of the majority of the group, because they wished to be accepted by them.

Zimbardo looked at how social roles have a powerful influence on behaviour. In this study, when young male students were randomly allocated to the role of either prisoner or guard, the allocated role influenced their behaviour. The guards became sadistic and oppressive and the prisoners became passive and depressed. Even when participants were unobserved, they conformed to their roles. Zimbardo concluded that role conformity was due to the social situation rather than to the personal characteristics of the participants, and that social roles have a powerful influence on behaviour.

Hofling studied obedience in a field experiment. Nurses working in a hospital were telephoned by an unknown doctor and asked to administer a drug to a patient. The doctor said he would sign the required paperwork later. To obey, the nurses would have to break hospital rules not to take telephone instructions and not to administer drugs unless the paperwork was completed. Twenty-one nurses obeyed the doctor and would have administered the drug had they not been stopped. The nurses said that they were often given instructions over the telephone and that doctors were annoyed if they refused. In this real-life setting in which doctors have high prestige, legitimate authority and power over nurses, obedience to authority was high.

Candidate B: AO2 section

In the Asch study, because there was a correct answer in the line-matching trials, conformity could be measured in an objective way allowing comparisons to be made. A strength of both Asch and Sherif is that these studies show us how a majority can influence an individual. However, a weakness of these controlled laboratory

experiments is that they do not show how people deal with situations that are important, and although the procedures in both these studies have internal validity they lack external realism. Also, both these experiments breach ethical guidelines as the participants did not give informed consent and were deceived. Psychologists should weigh the costs and benefits of unethical research before proceeding.

Zimbardo showed why people who have power may abuse this, but the artificial situation in this study may have led to demand characteristics where guards and prisoners may have been acting rather than conforming to their roles. Also in the Zimbardo study, the prisoners and guards were all young and about the same age. A real prison is an established social community in which the prisoners and guards do not all arrive at the same time; so compared to a real prison, the Zimbardo prison situation has low external validity.

Compared to the Milgram experiment, which was conducted in a specially contrived setting (in a laboratory), the advantage of the Hofling study is that this study was a field experiment carried out in a real hospital setting, giving it high external realism. Also, in Zimbardo and Milgram the all-male participants responded to advertisements and thus they were aware that they were being studied; but the Hofling sample, all female, were unaware that they were being studied, thus their behaviour was a more valid representation of how they would behave in their everyday lives. However, the Hofling study only concerns one kind of obedience, because nurses are trained to obey doctors, and thus it cannot be generalised to all other situations.

✍ Although both candidates A and B take a similar approach, there is a clear difference in the quality of these answers.

Candidate A gives a basic description in the AO1 section that demonstrates some relevant knowledge and understanding. There is some evidence of selection of material to address the question, but although the basic description of both Asch and Zimbardo is accurate, the candidate does not elaborate in any detail on what the findings/conclusions tell us about social influence. This part of the answer would probably be awarded 2–3 marks.

In the AO2 section the use of material provides only a basic commentary and superficial consideration of a restricted range of issues. Some specialist terms are used but the issues are not elaborated or fully explained. The candidate attempts to evaluate the quoted research and identifies issues but does not make clear the extent to which the research does or does not explain the processes of social influence. This part of the answer would probably be awarded 2 marks.

Candidate B makes an admirable selection of material in the AO1 section describing research into social influence. The candidate provides an accurate and detailed description of a wide range of appropriate research demonstrating sound knowledge and understanding. There is appropriate selection of material to address the question and the presentation is clear and coherent. The strength of this answer is that the candidate clearly understands what each study tells us about social influence. To save time, the candidate could have shortened the answer, because most candidates will struggle to write 300 words in 5–6 minutes. This part of the answer would probably be awarded 6 marks.

In the AO2 section the candidate has identified a broad range of issues and has commented on these issues in reasonable depth and in detail using appropriate evidence to support the arguments. There is a clear expression of ideas and the candidate uses a good range of psychological terms. One strength of this answer is that the candidate uses psychological terminology accurately to demonstrate that he/she has a good understanding of research methods and of the difficulty of drawing any firm conclusions from laboratory studies into social influence. Another strength of this answer is that through effective selection of material it focuses on the question 'as it is set'. Again, most candidates will struggle to write 300 words of AO2 commentary in 5–6 minutes, but this candidate has got the balance of AO1/AO2 right, which is important in this type of question. This part of the answer would probably attract 5–6 marks.

NB: Both the example answers first describe evidence and then evaluate the evidence, but you do not have to take this approach. An equally effective approach would be to describe and then evaluate evidence on a 'case by case' basis.

Individual differences (1)

Outline key features of the psychodynamic approach to psychopathology. (6 marks)

📝 **Question injunction = outline.** This question assesses **AO1 skills**, and marks are awarded if you demonstrate your understanding of the psychodynamic approach.

You could include:

- the role of the unconscious mind in motivating behaviour
- the theory that abnormal behaviour is caused by unresolved childhood conflict/early life experience
- the role of ego-defence mechanisms such as repression
- the theory of the tripartite human personality and fixation in stages of development

You are not expected to provide more than 5–6 minutes of writing.

■ ■ ■

Answers

Candidate A

The psychodynamic approach suggests that abnormal behaviour is motivated by unconscious forces and that the causes of abnormal behaviour lie in childhood. For example, failure to resolve the Oedipus or Electra conflict may cause psychological problems (e.g. Hans's phobia of horses).

Candidate B

The psychodynamic approach suggests that abnormal behaviour is motivated by unconscious forces and that the causes of abnormal behaviour lie in the past, usually in childhood, because repressed childhood conflict or anxiety may be triggered by events in adult life. For example, the psychoanalytic approach may suggest that an emotional disorder, such as depression, may be caused by the repression of unpleasant memories into the unconscious. This approach also theorises that unresolved conflict during the anal or phallic stage of development, when the ego is not fully developed, may result in ego-defence mechanisms of repression, projection or displacement.

📝 Although both answers are accurate, there is a clear difference in the quality of the answers.

Candidate A has given a basic outline demonstrating some relevant knowledge and understanding, but the answer could be more detailed. To improve this answer the candidate could have elaborated the example of the Oedipus conflict — at least to outline the stage of development in which this may occur. This answer would probably be awarded 2–3 marks.

Candidate B has given an accurate and detailed outline demonstrating relevant knowledge and understanding of the psychodynamic approach to psychopathology. There is appropriate selection of material to address the question. The strength of this answer is that the candidate has, using appropriate terminology, outlined appropriate examples of how the psychodynamic approach explains psychological problems. This answer would probably be awarded 5–6 marks.

Individual differences (2)

Explain how systematic desensitisation may overcome a fear of flying.   (6 marks)

📝 **Question injunction = explain.** This question assesses **AO2 skills,** and marks are awarded if you apply your knowledge and understanding to an unfamiliar situation. Your answer should include:

- a brief explanation of the process of systematic desensitisation
- an identification of elements in the hierarchy of fears
- how clients learn to associate pleasant relaxation with fear-provoking situations
- the step by step approach through the hierarchy of fears

Your answer must be explanatory rather than descriptive and you are not expected to provide more than 5–6 minutes of writing.

■ ■ ■

Answers

Candidate A

Based on the behavioural approach, systematic desensitisation helps people to gradually learn (conditioning) to associate a feared stimulus with a pleasant response such as relaxation.

Candidate B

Based on the behavioural approach, systematic desensitisation is based on learning (conditioning) to associate a feared stimulus with a pleasant response. During systematic desensitisation the undesirable behaviour (the phobia) is broken down into the small stimulus–response units that comprise it and these units are ranked into a hierarchy from least worrying to most fearful situation. In fear of flying the least fearful situation might be thinking about air travel when planning a holiday and the most feared situation might be boarding a plane. During therapy, the therapist first teaches the client to enjoy relaxation and then works though each stimulus–response unit in the hierarchy, from least feared stimulus to most feared stimulus, helping the person to replace each unwanted response of being afraid by the pleasure of feeling relaxed. If the therapy is successful, eventually the fear of flying will be eliminated.

📝 Although both answers are accurate there is a clear difference in the quality of the answers.

Candidate A has given a basic outline demonstrating some relevant knowledge and understanding, but the answer should be more detailed and much more clearly applied to fear of flying. This answer would probably be awarded 1–2 marks.

Candidate B has given an effective and accurate explanation of the process of systematic desensitisation and has applied this to fear of flying. The strength of this answer is that the candidate has, using appropriate terminology, explained the process of systematic desensitisation and has given an appropriate example of a possible hierarchy of fears of flying. This answer would probably be awarded 5–6 marks.

Individual differences (3)

Discuss the extent to which drug treatment is an effective and appropriate way to treat mental disorders. (6 marks)

Question injunction = discuss. This question assesses **AO2 skills**, and marks are awarded if you apply your knowledge and understanding of the appropriateness of drug treatment for mental disorders.

Your answer could include commentary on:
- the advantage of drug therapies that drug treatment can quickly relieve conditions such as depression and schizophrenia so that people are able to lead normal lives
- the advantage of drug treatment that it may allow a distressed patient to be well enough to receive psychological treatment
- the disadvantage of drug treatment that drugs may result in addiction or may cause unwanted side effects
- the disadvantage of drug treatment that drugs may hide the cause of the problem, which may re-occur when the patient stops taking the drug
- drug treatment being based on the assumption that psychological abnormality has an underlying biological cause
- the reductionist approach, because drug therapies ignore possible psychosocial factors involved in abnormal behaviour
- the ethical problems that arise when drug therapy is used to control behaviour that we do not understand

Your answer must be evaluative rather than descriptive and you should address the question of *effectiveness and appropriateness* of drug treatment. You are not expected to provide more than 5–6 minutes of writing.

■ ■ ■

Answers

Candidate A

Drug treatment is effective because it quickly relieves symptoms and enables people to live near-normal lives. Also, drug treatment is effective because taking drugs only requires the patient to remember to take the drugs, and does not involve changes of lifestyle. However, drugs cause side effects and may only provide temporary relief from symptoms, so when the patient stops taking the drugs the symptoms may recur. An advantage is that drug treatment can be used with psychological therapy. However, there may be individual differences in the effectiveness of drugs and in the quantity of side effects.

Candidate B

It can be argued that if the cause of mental illness is known to be biological, then drug treatment is appropriate and should be effective because drugs quickly relieve symptoms, enabling people to manage their lives more easily. For example, a benefit of antipsychotic drugs is that they are effective in helping psychotic patients to live near-'normal' lives. Another reason why drug treatment may be effective is that taking drugs, for example antidepressant tablets, only requires the patient to remember to take the drugs, and does not involve changes of lifestyle. However, unless there is a clearly understood biological cause for the problem, drug treatment may not be appropriate because drugs may only provide temporary relief from symptoms, and when the patient stops taking the drugs the symptoms may recur. A further problem is that it may be difficult to separate the effect of the drug from any placebo effect, so it may be difficult to gain a valid measure of the effectiveness of treatment. That said, an advantage of chemotherapy is that drugs can be used either to prepare people for, or together with, psychological therapies. Finally, ethical issues may arise because, if we do not know what effect a drug will have, it will be difficult to obtain fully informed consent to the treatment, and as each person may respond differently to the same drug treatment drug-induced side effects can be problematic.

🖉 Although both answers are accurate there is a clear difference in the quality of the answers.

Candidate A has provided a reasonable commentary, although the material is not always used effectively. A range of issues are evaluated in limited depth. The candidate expresses ideas using a range of specialist terms accurately and demonstrates some relevant knowledge and understanding. To improve this answer, she/he could have addressed the requirements of the question, *appropriateness and effectiveness*, with more clarity and by giving examples to illustrate the issues. This answer would probably be awarded 3–4 marks.

Candidate B has written a strong answer. The material is used effectively and a broad range of issues are evaluated in some depth. The candidate expresses ideas clearly using a range of specialist terms accurately to demonstrate relevant and sound knowledge and understanding. A strength of this answer is that the candidate clearly addresses the requirements of the question, *appropriateness and effectiveness*, and demonstrates understanding and application by giving examples to illustrate the issues. This answer would probably be awarded 5–6 marks.

Individual differences (4)

Explain one way psychologists have investigated the genetic basis of abnormality.

(4 marks)

📝 **Question injunction = explain.** This question assesses **AO3 skills,** and marks are awarded if you apply your knowledge and understanding of how psychologists investigate the genetic basis of psychological abnormality.

Your answer could include:
- twin studies and/or the study of biological relatives
- adoption studies

Explanations could focus on:
- assumptions about genetic similarity and the effect of shared environment
- conclusions that can or cannot be drawn from such studies
- the assumption that there is a biological basis for psychological abnormality

Your answer must be explanatory rather than descriptive and you are not expected to provide more than 4–5 minutes of writing.

■ ■ ■

Answers

Candidate A

Kety et al. (1994) looked at adoptees with chronic schizophrenia and found that the prevalence of the disorder was ten times higher in the biological relatives of the schizophrenic adoptees than in the biological relatives of the control group. This is evidence for the involvement of genetics in schizophrenia.

Candidate B

The biological approach assumes that psychological abnormality is possibly a symptom of some underlying genetic cause, and one way psychologists investigate this is by conducting twin studies. If a disorder is genetic, psychologists who conduct twin studies expect to find a higher concordance rate (the percentage of twins who, if their twin has a disorder, has the same disorder) in identical twins than in non-identical twins because identical twins are genetically identical. In family studies psychologists expect to find an increased risk of a disorder amongst first-degree relatives (parents, children and siblings) than in less genetically similar relatives.

📝 There is a clear difference in the quality of these answers.

Candidate A has not answered the question and has made the common error of providing a descriptive answer to a question asking for an explanation. Although he/she selected appropriate evidence there is no explanation as to why genetic similarity in twins predicts increased concordance rates in psychological abnormality. The answer would probably be awarded 1 mark.

Candidate B has left nothing to chance. The answer includes an accurate outline of the theoretical basis for twin studies as a means of investigating a genetic cause for psychological abnormality, and goes on to clearly explain what is predicted, if a disorder is genetic, in terms of the incidence of abnormality. Because the question asked for *'one way psychologists have investigated the genetic basis of abnormality'* the candidate did rather waste some time in the final commentary about family studies. The answer would probably be awarded 4 marks.